FOR NOBODY'S EYES ONLY

FOR NOBODY'S EYES ONLY

MISSING GOVERNMENT FILES AND HIDDEN ARCHIVES THAT DOCUMENT THE TRUTH BEHIND THE MOST ENDURING CONSPIRACY THEORIES

NICK REDFERN

A Division of The Career Press, Inc.
Pompton Plains, NJ

For Nobody's Eyes Only
Cover design by Howard Grossman/12E Design
Printed in the U.S.A.

To order this title, please call toll-free 1-800-CAREER-1 (NJ and Canada: 201-848-0310) to order using VISA or MasterCard, or for further information on books from Career Press.

The Career Press, Inc.
220 West Parkway, Unit 12
Pompton Plains, NJ 07444
www.careerpress.com

Library of Congress Cataloging-in-Publication Data

CIP Data Available Upon Request.

ACKNOWLEDGMENTS

I would like to offer my very sincere thanks and deep appreciation to everyone at New Page Books and Career Press, particularly Michael Pye, Laurie Kelly-Pye, Kirsten Dalley, Roger Sheety, Gina Talucci, Jeff Piasky, and Adam Schwartz; and to all the staff at Warwick Associates for their fine promotion and publicity campaigns. I would also like to say a very big thank you to my literary agent, Lisa Hagan, for all her hard work and help.

CONTENTS

INTRODUCTION

Mahatma Gandhi, the man who ultimately led India to gain independence from the United Kingdom, made a wise and knowing statement: "A small body of determined spirits fired by an unquenchable faith in their mission can alter the course of history." Gandhi's words were intended to be interpreted in a wholly positive fashion. That is to say, when people put their minds to tasks at hand, and their belief is solid, strong, and unswerving, they can achieve just about anything and everything they desire (Prabhu and Rao, 1998).

There is, however, another body of determined spirits who have an unquenchable faith in their mission and who can, and assuredly have, altered the course of history. They have done so in two most unfortunate ways: by hiding history and, sometimes, even by erasing it from the face of the Earth. And who might they be? They are nothing less than a small but influential body of characters secreted within the highest echelons of government. Following secret agendas, they have buried, burned, shredded, and hidden from the general public an incalculable number of Top Secret files that, if released and made available for one and all to see, would undoubtedly rewrite significant portions of 20th- and 21st-century history.

Government files and records get destroyed or denied release for all manner of reasons, not all of them, or even most of them, remotely sinister. And on this matter, it's vital, at the outset, to dispel some widely held views, opinions, assumptions, and prejudices. Often, conspiracy theorists point fingers at government agencies and, by default, practically accuse all of their collective employees of being implicated in countless cases of controversial chicanery and coverup. The reality is that the overwhelming majority of all employees of officialdom—whether of the CIA, the FBI, the National Security Agency, or of Britain's intelligence agencies, MI5 and MI6—are not engaged in any form of deceit, deception, and conspiracy. Indeed, the exact opposite is the case.

Most of those who work in the arena of government, and for whom high-level secrets are part and parcel of their everyday work, should not be demonized. They are loyal, patriotic individuals doing their utmost to defend their respective nations and people from enemies and aggressors. Unfortunately, the actions of the few often create situations that reflect upon, and sorely taint, the many. It is those few, those who wield significant power, and who sometimes operate outside of the law when the mood takes them or circumstances dictate is necessary, who we have in our sights in *For Nobody's Eyes Only*.

In the pages that follow, you will learn how, and why, the classified files on the infamous UFO crash at Roswell, New Mexico, in 1947 cannot be found. Anywhere. You'll also learn why not even the United States Congress, the Air Force, and the Government Accountability Office (the investigative arm of Congress) could locate the records pertaining to the alleged alien event. You'll come to appreciate how and why an almost identical situation applies to what might be termed a British Roswell. It's an out of this world incident that occurred in December 1980 that shook the British government to its foundations. Like Roswell, it's also a saga dominated by missing records and vanished files.

Moving away from UFOs, there are major questions to be answered, many of them relative to the world of Hollywood and famous faces. Why, for example, does the CIA deny holding any files on the world's most famous blond, Marilyn Monroe, when documented evidence from other agencies demonstrates the agency *does* have records on the legendary star? As for Diana, Princess of Wales—arguably one of the most famous faces of all time—who is it that sits tight on the hours upon hours of illegal recordings of her private phone calls with close confidantes and secret lovers?

What about classified government projects of a highly controversial nature? We're talking, specifically, about mind control, the use of human test subjects in radiation-based experiments, and even officialdom's deep digging into the dark and disturbing arena of black magic, Satanism, and the occult. We know the projects existed, but where are the records? Who is hiding them? Who destroyed them? Why is their very existence denied?

And speaking of missing records, the Watergate affair that brought down President Nixon, the November 1963 assassination of President John F. Kennedy, and the secret stash of files of legendary FBI boss, J. Edgar Hoover: They all fall under our scrutiny in the chapters that follow.

I started the Introduction to this book with a quote about history. So, it's only appropriate that I should finish the Introduction with one, too. It comes from Napoleon Bonaparte, the first emperor of France: "History is a set of lies that people have agreed upon" (Self-Made Myth, 2013).

PART 1:
WHAT SECRECY MEANS

1: WELCOME TO THE WORLD OF TOP SECRETS

To understand how and why government agencies classify data, it is important to have an appreciation of the nature of what constitutes classified material, as well as the various levels of secrecy that exist within officialdom and why. Often, the term "Top Secret" is recklessly tossed around by conspiracy theorists—usually in distinctly misleading style—to describe the contents of a particular file that is withheld by officialdom, or the circumstances surrounding an event that is considered to be deeply sensitive. In reality, most governments have systems in place that allow for documentation to be covered at *varying* degrees of classification, not just Top Secret. Those classifications depend on (a) the gravity of the particular material, and (b) the extent to which national security might be damaged if the data was released or compromised. And contrary to popular belief, there are no categories that are classified "above Top Secret." Rather, there are restricted access projects that, to gain entry to their inner sanctums, a person may be required to provide additional clearance in the form of a particular codeword. These operations are known as Special Access Programs, or SAPs. If it all sounds a bit confusing, well, read on.

SECRECY IN THE STATES

Let's begin with the United States of America. National security statutes and regulations are defined by what is termed an Executive Order of the President.

The most recent one—EO 13526—was passed on December 29, 2009, by President Barack Obama. The EO makes it clear that within the United States there are three specific levels of official secrecy: Top Secret, Secret, and Confidential. As for the highest degree of classification, we are told that: "Top Secret shall be applied to information, the unauthorized disclosure of which reasonably could be expected to cause exceptionally grave damage to the national security that the original classification authority is able to identify or describe." Material considered to be of Secret level is described in similar terms to those which apply to Top Secret status, except that, whereas the unauthorized release of Top Secret material may cause "*grave* damage" to U.S. national security, Secret material leaked outside of official channels might provoke "*serious* damage." Regarding the Confidential category, this is the lowest level of secrecy in the United States' military, government, and intelligence arenas. Even so, EO 13526 makes it clear that significant damage to security of the nation could still occur if data of a Confidential level was compromised and shared with hostile forces (Executive Order 13526—Classified National Security Information, 2009).

As for the particular topics that fall under the umbrella of EO 13526, they include: (a) Army, Navy, and Air Force strategies and programs; (b) the current state of U.S. military capabilities; (c) information on overseas—and potentially—enemy nations; (d) the means by which the U.S. government

The National Archives, Maryland, is home to millions of pages of formerly classified files. ©Nick Redfern

secures intelligence-based data; (e) the names and locations of both domestic and foreign covert sources of material; (f) the ways America can defend its nuclear arsenals; and (g) matters relative to one of the biggest, potential problems facing the free world today: weapons of mass destruction (WMDs).

DECLASSIFICATION AND NON-DECLASSIFICATION

It is a fallacy to assume that all documentation, regardless of its level of secrecy, ultimately gets declassified by those U.S. agencies that are withholding it or have jurisdiction over it. EO 13526 makes it clear that at the time the security level of a particular document is decided upon, "the original classification authority shall establish a specific date or event for declassification based on the duration of the national security sensitivity of the information." If, however, the person or persons who determined whether a particular file should be stamped Confidential, Secret, or Top Secret cannot decide upon a particular time when declassification should occur, "information shall be marked for declassification 10 years from the date of the original decision, unless the original classification authority otherwise determines that the sensitivity of the information requires that it be marked for declassification for up to 25 years from the date of the original decision" (Executive Order 13526—Classified National Security Information, 2009).

As for any data that might be considered important enough to be withheld for more than a quarter of a century, this requires certain "standards and procedures for classifying information" to be carefully studied. This, generally at least, revolves around the important question of: How damaging to national security might it be to release the relevant file, regardless of its ever-increasing age? As a result, files can, and assuredly do, get withheld for more than 25 years. Nevertheless, as the documentation that President Obama put into place on December 29, 2009, makes clear: "No information may remain classified indefinitely" (Ibid.). Technically, that is completely true. But, even so, there are still a number of means and methods by which data can remain outside of the public domain for decades, even lifetimes. Let's look at the facts on the matter.

Section 3.3 of EO 13526, titled *Automatic Declassification*, informs government personnel that: "...all classified records that (1) are more than 25 years old and (2) have been determined to have permanent historical value...shall be automatically declassified whether or not the records have been reviewed." That is, theoretically, in the year that the book you are now reading was published, 2013, every single document ever produced by the U.S. government up until

1988 should now be in the public domain. Then, in 2014, the 1989 files should be declassified. Well, sometimes it works like that, but certainly not always. Although millions of pages of formerly classified files can be accessed in person at the National Archives, in College Park, Maryland, there is a particular clause contained within Section 3.3 of EO 13526 that has a major bearing upon this 25-year-long period of limitation on what we can, or often cannot, be allowed to see (Ibid.).

The clause in question allows the directors of government agencies the ability and right to deny the public and the media access to files that are older than 25 years, providing certain criteria are met. Those criteria cover, as one would expect, a wealth of critical national security–themed matters, including such issues as U.S. military technology, sources and methods of gathering intelligence data, safety issues surrounding the president and his staff, plans for war, and relations with overseas nations, both friendly and aggressive. As a result, and on many occasions, a period of 25 years is not the end of the line, after all. And should anyone within government decide to sidestep these regulations, and surreptitiously share secret files with outsiders, he or she can end up in deep trouble. It may even mean spending the rest of his or her days securely locked in a small room in Guantanamo Bay.

TALKING OUT OF TURN

One of the actions that the U.S. government can take against those employees that do leak classified material is to invoke the Espionage Act of 1917, which was signed into law by President Woodrow Wilson. A little-known piece of legislation that, as its name suggests, is now almost a century old, it is still in regular use to this day. Certainly, one of the most visible examples of how the act has been used in recent years is in the case of Bradley Manning, a U.S. Army soldier who was placed under arrest in May 2010 for passing classified materials on to WikiLeaks, the controversial and notorious body overseen by the equally controversial Australian Julian Assange. Two years later, in 2012, a former CIA officer named John Kiriakou was charged under the terms of the same act for sharing secret information with journalists on matters relative to undercover agents involved in crushing al-Qaeda.

Secrets, as all the above shows, are a fact of life in government. They are also guarded and maintained with the utmost zeal. Sometimes, however, secrets are allowed to enter the public domain, as we shall now see.

2: FREEDOM OF INFORMATION AND NEED TO KNOW

It was on Independence Day 1966 that President Lyndon B. Johnson signed an historic piece of documentation that brought into being the Freedom of Information Act (FOIA). The FOIA permits members of the general public and the media the right to file a request with government agencies to (a) obtain copies of files that may already be declassified, or (b) request that files which are currently withheld—either in whole or in part—be declassified into the public arena. The FOIA, however, is not a tool that is guaranteed to open all doors. There are many clauses within the act that permit government, military, and intelligence-based bodies to withhold their files, if they deem it appropriate to do so. The grounds for denial of access to files via the FOIA include national security concerns, matters having a bearing on the defense of the nation, privacy issues, data relative to legal and criminal subjects, and the internal operations of the relevant agency or agencies.

As all of the above shows, although there certainly are ways and means by which government-based Top Secret files may be declassified, there are also stringent laws available that allow for the continued non-disclosure of records for many years—decades, in some cases, and particularly so where agency chiefs have deemed the papers to be extremely sensitive. It's much the same in other countries, too.

SECRETS OF THE OFFICIAL KIND

In the same, precise way that official documentation in the United States is subject to varying levels of secrecy, such is also the situation in the UK. The classifications in Britain are, in rising order of importance: Unclassified, Protect, Restricted, Confidential, Secret, and Top Secret.

In the UK, a piece of legislation exists that is designed to prevent certain employees of Her Majesty's government from breaching security and sharing classified materials with non-cleared individuals. It is called the Official Secrets Act (OSA). Those that fall under the auspices of the OSA are termed Crown Servants. This includes members of the Royal Navy, Royal Air Force, and British Army, as well as employees of British Intelligence, such as MI5 (the UK's version of the FBI), MI6 (Britain's CIA), and the Government Communications Headquarters (the British equivalent of the United States' National Security Agency). Prosecution under the terms of the OSA, for such actions as revealing the contents of classified documents, can result in lengthy prison sentences, particularly if potentially dangerous damage to national security *could* have resulted, *has* resulted, or, in the future, still *might* result.

As far as the general public's right to access official documentation in the UK is concerned, this used to fall under the banner of what was called the Thirty Year Rule, a 1958 creation of the British Parliament. As its title implies, the Thirty Year Rule ensured that all government records, regardless of their level of sensitivity, remained behind closed doors until a period of 30 years had passed since their creation. At that point, they were flagged for review by the agency that possessed them, after which they could have been released and made available to one and all. Or not. The vast majority of those now-visible files are housed at the National Archives, a huge building situated in Kew, England, which acts as the primary resource facility for public access to official records in the UK.

At the turn of the 21st century, however, everything changed. The Labor Government of the day passed the Freedom of Information Act 2000, which followed broadly similar guidelines to those present in the United States' FOIA. The British people no longer had to wait 30 years to see certain government files. The ability to continue to deny access to old records for matters relative to national security and the defense of the realm, however, was still in place.

A glance at the rest of the world shows that many developed nations have followed in the tracks of both the United States and the UK. For example, Canada, India, and New Zealand have Official Secrets Acts. Freedom of Information laws apply in numerous nations, including Australia, Brazil, Canada, Denmark, France, Mexico, Norway, Sweden, and Turkey. Like Britain and the

*The United Kingdom's National Archives, where once-secret papers are now on display.
©Nick Redfern*

United States, all of the above countries have laws that permit agencies to keep files under lock and key as they see fit, providing that justification is seen as being firmly warranted.

SPECIAL ACCESS AND NEED TO KNOW

As noted in the previous chapter, contrary to what is often assumed—or claimed by alleged whistleblowers of distinctly dubious credibility—there are absolutely no levels of secrecy that extend beyond Top Secret. Not a single one. That does not mean, however, that having a Top Secret clearance provides a person with carte-blanche access to every secret, every conspiracy, and every cover-up under the face of the Sun. In fact, quite the opposite is the general rule of thumb. Here we come to something termed "need to know." Person "A" might have the same level of clearance—let's say Top Secret—as person "B." But here's the important point: To protect the security and secrecy of the project on which "A" is working, he or she is given a classified piece of data that acts as a key to open the door to that same project. That key might be in the form of a piece of documentation, such as a sternly worded, non-disclosure agreement.

Alternately, it might be a classified codeword that, without which, access to the program would be denied at all times. So we have a situation where "A" and "B" possess the exact same clearance level of Top Secret, but only "A" knows what is afoot in the classified world of "Project X." Such "Project X"–type operations are termed SAPs (Special Access Programs).

In the United States, where SAPs are far more prevalent than anywhere else, they primarily relate to (a) the "research, development, testing, modification, and evaluation or procurement" of new and sophisticated technologies; (b) the "planning and execution of especially sensitive intelligence" operations; and (c) the "execution and support" of classified military programs. It is within the arena of SAPs that some of the most guarded of all secrets remain deeply buried (Executive Order 13526—Classified National Security Information, 2009).

And, while we're on the subject of some of the most guarded, official secrets of all time—and how and why governments withhold reams of secret documents from public view—let's now take a careful and close look at a wealth of world events, incidents, and affairs where missing papers, denied documents, hidden archives, burned files, and shredded dossiers absolutely abound. Collectively, these are the most interesting, amazing, controversial, and dangerous files of all. They are the files that are deemed for nobody's eyes only. We'll start with a tale of, quite possibly, other-world proportions.

PART 2:
UFOS, ALIENS, AND
COSMIC CONSPIRACIES

3: THE ROSWELL FILES: ABDUCTED!

The July 8, 1947, edition of the New Mexico–based *Roswell Daily Record* newspaper had a bold and dynamic headline that quickly caught the eyes of amazed locals. It read: "RAAF Captures Flying Saucer on Ranch in Roswell Region." It sensationally revealed that military personnel from the town's Roswell Army Air Force (the RAAF, as it was known back then) had obtained an honest-to-goodness flying saucer. No, this was not a case of someone getting confused and thinking it was April 1st. And yes, the military was talking about a real flying saucer. The RAAF's Press Information Officer, Walter Haut, prepared a press release on the affair and the excited editor of the *Daily Record* wasted no time in unleashing its contents upon the town and its people:

The many rumors regarding the flying disc became a reality yesterday when the Intelligence office of the 509th Bomb Group of the Eighth Air Force, Roswell Army Air Field, was fortunate to gain possession of a disc through the cooperation of one of the local ranchers and the sheriff's office of Chaves County. The flying object landed on a ranch near Roswell sometime last week. Not having phone facilities, the rancher stored the disc until such time as he was able to contact the sheriff's office, who in turn notified Maj. Jesse A. Marcel of the 509th Bomb Group Intelligence Office. Action was immediately taken and the disc was picked up at the rancher's home. It was inspected at the Roswell Army Air Field and subsequently loaned by Major Marcel to higher headquarters ("RAAF Captures Flying Saucer On Ranch in Roswell Region," July 8, 1947).

The undeniably mysterious event actually occurred about a 90 minutes' drive from Roswell, on a remote and huge slab of Lincoln County, New Mexico, farmland called the Foster Ranch. It has subsequently become the subject of dozens of non-fiction books, a number of science-fiction novels, official studies undertaken by both the Government Accountability Office and the U.S. Air Force, a plethora of television documentaries, a movie starring Martin Sheen and Kyle MacLachlan, and considerable media scrutiny of a distinctly pro and decidedly con nature. The affair has also left in its wake a near mountain of theories to explain the event, including a weather balloon; a Mogul balloon secretly utilized to monitor for Soviet atomic bomb tests; an extraterrestrial spacecraft; a series of dark and dubious high-altitude exposure experiments using human beings; some sort of near catastrophic atomic mishap; the crash of a Nazi V-2 rocket with shaved monkeys on board; a Soviet experiment involving a futuristic aircraft and grossly mutated children; and an accident that revolved around an aerial contraption secretly built by transplanted German scientists who had relocated to the United States following the end of the Second World War.

A BALLOON BURSTS WHILE A SAUCER VANISHES

Whatever the truth of the matter of Roswell, and the ultimate point of origin of the craft and its strange crew, it is an undeniable fact that the military hastily and decisively retracted its sensational statement that had appeared on the front page of the *Roswell Daily Record*, preferring, instead, to substitute it for a far more down to earth and prosaic one. It was asserted by the top brass that the personnel from the Roswell Army Air Force base had made a spectacular error: The materials originated not with a futuristic disc from another planet, after all, but with nothing stranger than an ordinary, mundane weather balloon. From a flying saucer to a weather balloon, that's a hell of a difference. And, if it was only a simple weather balloon, then why were the military elite of Roswell not able to recognize the device as such in the first place? After all, one does not have to be a rocket scientist to recognize a balloon when one sees it. On top of that, staff at the base launched weather balloons every day of the week.

Despite the best attempts of officials to lay the perplexing matter to rest, it is questions like the one above that ensure the Roswell enigma shows no signs

The Foster Ranch, New Mexico: the site of the legendary UFO crash of 1947. ©Nick Redfern

of going away any time soon. And there's something else, too. According to the story that has developed since, the Foster Ranch was reportedly cordoned off, dozens of military personnel were assigned to guard the site and recover both the wreckage and a number of stinking, decomposing bodies of undetermined origin, and the entire kit and caboodle was reportedly retrieved under great secrecy. At least some of this priceless material, as Walter Haut's press release made clear, was then subsequently "loaned" to what was described as a "higher headquarters." The final destination of the whatever-it-was, many UFO researchers conclude—based on interviews with military old-timers— was the Foreign Technology Division at Wright Field, Ohio, today known as Wright-Patterson Air Force Base ("RAAF Captures Flying Saucer on Ranch in Roswell Region," July 8, 1947).

One would imagine that, with all of this hectic, secret activity going on, someone, somewhere, would surely have officially documented each and every aspect of the entire affair. Yet, today, all we have on the Roswell event are a couple of scraps of official documentation and, well, that's about it. Regardless of whatever happened significant miles from Roswell, the voluminous files that surely should have been generated on an affair in which the U.S. military played a major role are missing, lost, unavailable, buried. Call it what you will, but, at the end of the day, it all comes down to just one thing: *The records have vanished into oblivion.*

But, to where, exactly?

Forty-six years after *something* came down on the Foster Ranch, one man tried valiantly and diligently to find the answers behind Roswell and the elusive documentation. In doing so he opened up a definitive can of worms and shed a significant amount of light on the matter of those missing files.

A CONGRESSMAN WANTS THE FILES BUT GETS THE RUNAROUND

In early 1993, United States Congressman Steven Schiff began probing into the many complexities of the Roswell affair. His first port of call, as he sought out the files on the controversial saga, was the Department of Defense. In a March 11, 1993, letter to Secretary of Defense Les Aspin, Schiff explained that during the previous fall he "became aware of a strange series of events beginning in New Mexico over 45 years ago and involving personnel of what was then the Army Air Force." It was specifically on the matter of this "strange series of events" that Schiff wanted answers. And he wanted them soon. Thus began an inquiry that ultimately led to major, official revelations concerning missing, and unaccounted for, files on the Roswell controversy (Schiff, March 11, 1993).

Three weeks later, Schiff's office received a reply from Colonel Larry G. Shockley who, at the time, was the U.S. Air Force's director of plans and operations. The only action taken by Shockley was to refer Congressman Schiff to the Maryland-based National Archives, which, like its British counterpart at Kew, is home to millions of pages of formerly classified U.S. government files. This hardly satisfied the congressman, because his staff had *already* been able to determine that there was absolutely nothing relative to the Roswell mystery held at the National Archives. Schiff began to wonder if, even at this early stage, he was being given the runaround. His suspicions may have been right on target.

AGAIN, AGAIN, AND AGAIN

Far from pleased by simply being deceived and referred to the National Archives for answers, Schiff fired off another letter to the Department of Defense, demanding to specifically know what the DoD, and *not* the National Archives, knew about Roswell. The reply came from Rudy de Leon, the special Assistant to the secretary of defense. De Leon told the congressman that although he admitted to personally finding the controversy on the mysterious crash intriguing, and because any theoretical files that might exist from Roswell would be decades old by 1993, they would no longer be stored at de Leon's place of work, which was the Pentagon. Somewhat outrageously, de Leon added that if

Schiff wanted answers, and any attendant files on Roswell, he should go knocking on the door of the National Archives. *Again*!

Schiff, further angered that matters appeared to be going around in circles and nowhere else at all, did not go back to the National Archives. Instead, he continued to hammer, ever harder, upon the heavily guarded doors of the Pentagon. In forthright tones, Schiff detailed the situation to Secretary of Defense Les Aspin. Again!

Schiff explained that it was pointless to keep referring him to staff at the National Archives and to no one else. "Wherever the documents may be," Schiff forthrightly told Aspin, "what is at issue is my request for a personal briefing and a written report on a matter involving actions taken by officials of the U.S. Army and U.S. Air Force, agencies under your purview. I realize the research required to uncover the relevant documents and related materials will take time and considerable effort, and I am prepared to wait a reasonable amount of time for this to be accomplished." Schiff added, just for good measure, and to make sure the Pentagon knew he wasn't going away quietly or anytime soon: "I expect the job to be done" (Schiff, 1993).

Schiff was almost dumbstruck by the reply he received. It didn't come from Aspin or his staff. Instead, it came from our old friends at the National Archives! Despite the fact that a by now seriously vexed Schiff had made it clear, in his latest communication to Aspin, that personnel at the archives had been at pains to point out they had nothing on file regarding Roswell, Aspin's staff simply ignored his words and put the ball in the National Archives' court. Again!

Any doubts that Schiff might have had on the matter of being stonewalled were now gone. He was now a man firmly on a mission to find the holiest of all holy grails: the original records that documented what really happened deep in the New Mexico desert in July 1947. When Schiff's next letter to the Department of Defense went unanswered for an amazing three months, his office, fuming with anger, took matters to a whole different level. If silence was now the only thing that could be expected from staff of the DoD, it was time to bring in a significant degree of powerful back-up. It came in the form of the Government Accountability Office (or the General Accounting Office, as it was known in 1993 and up until its name change in 2004), which is the investigative arm of the United States Congress.

GETTING THE REINFORCEMENTS INVOLVED IN ROSWELL

Congressman Schiff personally spoke with the GAO's controller general, Charles A. Bowsher, and complained how the DoD—after first stonewalling and then near-endlessly and stubbornly referring him to the National Archives and to no one else—was now being unresponsive to his inquiries on Roswell. Schiff went public, too, telling the media that, although he was fairly skeptical on the matter of aliens and flying saucers, he had to admit that the weather balloon scenario seemed not to hold water—hence his demand for an investigation.

Schiff made no bones about how he felt regarding the treatment dished out to him by the DoD, and called the lack of action, and the undeniable runaround that he and his staff received, "astounding." An angry Schiff added to the press: "If the Defense Department had been responsive, it wouldn't have come to this." But come to this it most assuredly had. And when the GAO got involved in a quest to seek out the hidden or missing Roswell files, it wasn't so much what did surface that was intriguing, but what didn't surface (Claiborne, 1994).

ROSWELL FILES? WHAT ROSWELL FILES?

On July 28, 1995, almost two years after Congressman Schiff approached his staff, the Government Accountability Office's report on the Roswell affair surfaced from its National Security and International Affairs Division. The GAO, to its lasting credit, spent more than a year digging deeply into the Roswell controversy. In doing so, it requested numerous agencies—including the CIA, the FBI, the Air Force, the National Security Agency, and the Defense Intelligence Agency—to check their archives for everything on Roswell. Aside from a scant couple of one- and two-page documents from the FBI and the military, none of which offered any kind of adequate, meaningful insight on the truth behind the legend—and all of which had already been declassified to UFO researchers, via FOIA, *decades* earlier—nothing else surfaced at all.

For all intents and purposes, the Roswell files might just as well have been abducted, somewhat appropriately, by aliens. But it was not just the documents on the incident itself that were missing. During their search for records to understand what had really taken place in New Mexico in early July 1947, the GAO learned that a massive amount of official documentation generated from within the confines of the Roswell Army Air Force between March 1945 and December 1949 had vanished, too. Moreover, that same documentation had disappeared under questionable circumstances. When GAO investigators asked for an explanation, they were told by the chief archivist for the National Personnel Records Center that its staff had been unable to ascertain how, why, and under whose jurisdiction the files had vanished.

Speculation was rife within UFO research circles that the U.S. government was being overly careful and, by removing at some undetermined point whole swathes of records from 1945 to 1949, wanted to make sure that (a) nothing incriminating was left behind and (b) nothing of relevance had been misplaced in an *earlier* collection of material, or indeed, within a *later* body of data, possibly held in secure safes at the old base at Roswell. So, ufologists suggested, those people who were tasked with keeping the truth of Roswell hidden, chose the best and quickest option available to them. They scooped up everything that covered approximately two years or so before, and up to two and a half years after, the crash. Maybe, that is exactly what happened. And maybe it was done not just to keep UFO investigators in the dark, but even the GAO and Congressman Schiff. I say "maybe" because, even to this day, no satisfactory explanation has surfaced officially on the matter of those missing 1945 to 1949 papers. But whatever the answer, we're still not done with the missing files of Roswell.

THE AIR FORCE KNOWS BEST, SAYS WHO? THE AIR FORCE!

In a very curious move, instead of simply answering the GAO's questions about Roswell, and searching diligently for any and all official documentation that might exist on the case, the Air Force instead chose to jump the gun and quickly launched its own investigation of the mysterious crash. Needless to say, this angered certain figures within the GAO, since *they* represented the investigating agency, and the Air Force's sole mandate in the matter was just to respond to its—the GAO's—inquiries and requests, and share any uncovered data that might have been found. Despite giving Congressman Schiff headaches when he asked for answers about Roswell, it didn't take any time before the Air Force had an answer regarding what really happened on the Foster Ranch all those years earlier. The GAO, in its report, stated that the Air Force "concluded that there was no dispute that something happened near Roswell in July 1947 and that all available official materials indicated the most likely source of the wreckage recovered was one of the project MOGUL balloon trains. At the time of the Roswell crash, Project MOGUL was a highly classified U.S. effort to determine the state of Soviet nuclear weapons research using balloons that carried radar reflectors and acoustic sensors" (General Accounting Office, 1995).

That's all fine and dandy, except for one amazing thing: There were no "available official materials." Yes, as the Air Force dug into its many archives, it *did* uncover thousands of pages of documentation on the Mogul program. And, yes, many of those documents *were* originally classified, some at a high

level, too. Not one of the papers, however, made any kind of reference whatsoever to the recovery of any Mogul materials at the Foster Ranch in the summer
of 1947. In other words, the Air Force's "most likely" conclusion was not based
on a study of very old, smoking-gun-style documentation that it had stumbled
upon, but on supposition, opinion, and theory. If files did once exist to show
that what was found on the Foster Ranch were the remains of a Mogul balloon,
then they had vanished as mysteriously as had the countless records from the
Roswell Army Air Field covering 1945 to 1949. But why would someone have
destroyed, or carefully secreted away from prying eyes, files on the crash of
nothing stranger than a Mogul balloon on the Foster Ranch, when thousands
of additional pages of Mogul-themed papers were found by the Air Force, and
duly declassified into the public domain, as part of its attempt to solve the
puzzle of Roswell? Nothing about the Air Force's explanation made any sense.
Then there's the pesky, and not insignificant, matter of those mysterious, decaying little bodies that were reportedly found at the crash site (Ibid.).

DOES THE GOVERNMENT THINK WE'RE DUMMIES?

The Air Force's 1994 report on Roswell was notable for one other thing
beyond its Mogul explanation for what happened. It was the almost complete
lack of any attempt to try to adequately explain away the stories of corpses—
human, animal, alien, or something else—found at the crash site and transferred to secure military installations for preservation, autopsy, and study. The
Air Force's reasoning and logic for this was that, because Mogul balloons did
not have crews, and a Mogul balloon was the cause of the Roswell legend, there
was no need for them to address the matter of bodies. That situation changed
drastically, and curiously, in the summer of 1997, when the Air Force came up
with a second report on Roswell. Three years on, the Air Force decided that
bodies, of a sort anyway, *were* found. In contrast to the first report, this new one
focused almost exclusively on the bodies.

Titled *The Roswell Report: Case Closed*, the document was published as
interest in the story reached fever-pitch levels. The reason for this was simple
yet memorable: The summer of 1997 just happened to mark the 50th anniversary of the notoriously weird event. The Air Force's timing was intriguing
and guaranteed to generate a great deal of publicity, which it did. But its new
report did nothing to quash the atmosphere of overwhelming and profound
conspiracy that had come to famously define Roswell. In fact, it had the marked
distinction of achieving the exact opposite.

Prepared by Captain James McAndrew, who was an intelligence applications Officer assigned to the Secretary of the Air Force Declassification and Review Team at the Pentagon, the 213-page report came to a controversial conclusion:

> *Aliens' observed in the New Mexico desert were probably anthropomorphic test dummies that were carried aloft by U.S. Air Force high altitude balloons for scientific research. The "unusual" military activities in the New Mexico desert were high altitude research balloon launch and recovery operations. The reports of military units that always seemed to arrive shortly after the crash of a flying saucer to retrieve the saucer and "crew," were actually accurate descriptions of Air Force personnel engaged in anthropomorphic dummy recovery operations (McAndrew, 1997).*

The most important word in the quote above is "probably." It might even have been the most important word in the entire report. Why? Just as with its Mogul report of 1994, the Air Force could not find any official documentation to support the theory that crash-test dummies were really the source of the "alien bodies" legends from Roswell. The conclusions were all based on guesswork, assumption, and theory. There's no doubt that the military *did* engage in high-altitude, balloon-based experiments in New Mexico. And there's no doubt that although of those same experiments involved the use of human-sized dummies, as well as some dummies of a shorter stature. The problem, however, is that while the Air Force's response, *The Roswell Report: Case Closed*, provided lots of nice photos of crash-test dummies, and mountains of documentation, none of this collective material dated from 1947. Nor did it in any way relate to events that had occurred on a certain now-infamous ranch. There's a good reason for that: The dummy experiments did not even begin until 1953, which was more than half a decade after the Roswell crash occurred (Ibid.).

The Air Force's response, when the mainstream media latched onto this notable fact, came from Colonel John Haynes. Placed on the proverbial spot, Haynes, clearly displaying on-screen awkwardness, said at a press conference that highlighted the new report: "I don't know what they saw in '47, but I'm quite sure it probably was Project MOGUL. But I think if you find that people talk about things over a period of time, they begin to lose exactly when the date was" (CNN Larry King Live, 2003). Evidently, that goes for the Air Force, too, because it claimed that experiments which began in 1953 were responsible for aspects of an event that occurred in 1947. Unless those dummies were time-travelers, it seems safe to conclude that the Air Force's best guesstimate was very wide off the mark. And even if one or two such crash-test-dummy-based experiments did occur in 1947, and were responsible for the tales of alien bodies found at Roswell, why should all the relevant documentation be missing, when *from every other year in which the program existed* the files have been found and declassified.

THE ROSWELL "RAT"

On April 1, 2011, the FBI unleashed upon the world a huge, new Website. Its name is the Vault. Following a radical shake-up of its original FBI Records/Freedom of Information and Privacy Act Website one year earlier, the new site was designed to provide eager readers with access to thousands of previously classified Bureau documents that "have been scanned from paper into digital copies so you can read them in the comfort of your own home or office" ("FBI Records: The Vault," 2011).

The Vault does indeed provide literally hundreds of thousands of pages of once-withheld files on all manner of people and topics, including actress Marilyn Monroe, scientist Albert Einstein, gangsters Bonnie and Clyde, the Civil Rights Movement, Watergate, and the June 1968 assassination of Robert F. Kennedy. And all the files can be downloaded quickly and easily in PDF format. In terms of government openness, this is an excellent and praiseworthy move. There's just one problem, however: Several of the files that were deleted from the FBI's original Website were not transferred to the Vault. One of those files, interestingly enough, was on a key and controversial player in the Roswell saga.

Philip Corso served in the U.S. Army from February 1942 until March 1963 and retired with the rank of lieutenant colonel. In 1997, 34 years after his military career ended, Corso provoked a storm of debate when a sensational book that he co-authored with William Birnes, the co-editor of *UFO Magazine*, was published. The title of the book was *The Day After Roswell*. The controversial story told of Corso's alleged personal knowledge of the Roswell affair while serving with the military. The book also described the way in which he, Corso, allegedly helped to advance the United States—both scientifically and militarily—by secretly feeding certain fantastic technologies found in the alien craft recovered at Roswell in 1947 to American-based private industries and defense contractors. Without the recovered Roswell artifacts and his personal actions, maintained Corso, both loudly and proudly, there would be no fiber-optics, no night-vision equipment, no computers as we know them today, no high-powered lasers; the list was almost never-ending, as were Corso's fantastic revelations.

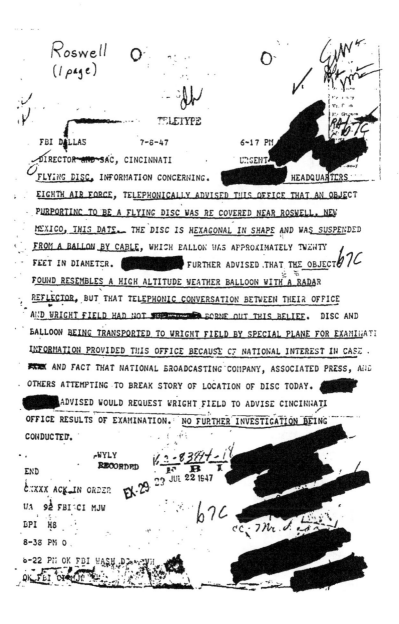

Roswell
(1 page)

TELETYPE

FBI DALLAS   7-8-47   6-17 PM

DIRECTOR AND SAC, CINCINNATI   URGENT

FLYING DISC, INFORMATION CONCERNING.   HEADQUARTERS

EIGHTH AIR FORCE, TELEPHONICALLY ADVISED THIS OFFICE THAT AN OBJECT
PURPORTING TO BE A FLYING DISC WAS RE COVERED NEAR ROSWELL, NEW
MEXICO, THIS DATE. THE DISC IS HEXAGONAL IN SHAPE AND WAS SUSPENDED
FROM A BALLON BY CABLE, WHICH BALLON WAS APPROXIMATELY TWENTY
FEET IN DIAMETER.   FURTHER ADVISED THAT THE OBJECT
FOUND RESEMBLES A HIGH ALTITUDE WEATHER BALLOON WITH A RADAR
REFLECTOR, BUT THAT TELEPHONIC CONVERSATION BETWEEN THEIR OFFICE
AND WRIGHT FIELD HAD NOT   BORNE OUT THIS BELIEF. DISC AND
BALLOON BEING TRANSPORTED TO WRIGHT FIELD BY SPECIAL PLANE FOR EXAMINATI
INFORMATION PROVIDED THIS OFFICE BECAUSE OF NATIONAL INTEREST IN CASE.
AND FACT THAT NATIONAL BROADCASTING COMPANY, ASSOCIATED PRESS, AND
OTHERS ATTEMPTING TO BREAK STORY OF LOCATION OF DISC TODAY.
ADVISED WOULD REQUEST WRIGHT FIELD TO ADVISE CINCINNATI
OFFICE RESULTS OF EXAMINATION. NO FURTHER INVESTIGATION BEING
CONDUCTED.

               WYLY
               RECORDED
END
EXXX ACK IN ORDER
UA 92 FBI CI MJW
EPI H8
8-38 PM O
6-22 PM OK FBI WASH D
OK FBI CI MJE

*An FBI document on the mysterious Roswell affair of July 1947. ©Federal Bureau of
Investigation, 1947*

Within UFO research circles, deep divisions over Corso's claims quickly surfaced when *The Day After Roswell* appeared. Some UFO investigators felt that Corso's story was 100 percent true. Others mused that it was all a big joke on the part of Corso, one that was designed to elevate him to superstar status and bring in a good amount of money in his old age. And then there was the theory that the story was government-created disinformation, designed to cloud the controversial truth concerning what did or did not occur in the New Mexico desert all those decades ago. In this latter, hypothetical scenario, Corso secretly agreed to be the man to disseminate the disinformation. One of the steps that industrious UFO researchers took to try to ascertain the truth about Corso's claims was to file Freedom of Information requests with the FBI for any files that might have existed on the man. It turns out the FBI did have a file on Corso. And as a result of the requests, the file was soon uploaded to the FBI's Website for all to view. But, when the FBI began the lengthy process of transferring its declassified files from its original site to the Vault, the Corso file failed to make the transition. Fortunately, however, I downloaded the file from the original site before it vanished.

Though the document package does not contain any smoking guns relative to the Roswell affair, it does reveal a few things that Corso had to say on one highly sensitive matter that intrigued him: the JFK assassination of November 1963, another conspiratorial affair dominated by missing and sealed files, as will become clear in Chapter 15 of this book. One particular document contained in the file—dated February 11, 1965, and sent from FBI employee M.A. Jones to Cartha DeLoach, a former assistant director of the FBI—reveals what Corso had to say on the assassination and what the FBI thought of the man and his character:

> *Bufiles contain a number of references to Corso.... He has contacted the FBI from time to time, especially in the 1940s, usually in connection with some allegation concerning the subversive activity of one individual or another. Corso was also alleged to be responsible for putting out a rumor that Lee Harvey Oswald was an FBI informant. When interviewed on 2-10-64, by you [DeLoach] regarding this, Corso indicated his 'sources in CIA had merely presumed that Oswald was an informant for the FBI.' When you challenged him to identify his CIA sources, Corso repeatedly failed to produce names. There is good reason to believe Corso never got such information from CIA and the 'deductions' were his own. The Director noted: 'Corso is a rat'(Jones, 1965).*

The document continues to paint an unflattering portrait of Corso:

From your [DeLoach's] interview with Corso on 2-10-64, you got the definite impression that he was a rather shifty-eyed individual who fancied himself a great intelligence expert.... He stressed his sources had no facts but that their belief Oswald was an FBI informant merely stemmed from idle deduction during a conversation. He said he was responsible for leading this discussion in this regard because of his extensive experiences with military intelligence; he felt that any American citizen who was given a job in the Soviet Union, allowed to marry a Soviet citizen and then permitted to return with her to the U.S., could only be an FBI or CIA informant (Ibid.).

THE DAY AFTER A FILE VANISHES

Thus, for the man who claimed to know the truth about the Roswell cover-up, he was also alluding to the idea that there was some sort of conspiracy behind the killing of President John F. Kennedy, and that Lee Harvey Oswald was far more than just a lone patsy, as he has become memorably known. Regardless of how one views the killing of JFK and the not-so-positive image of Corso as portrayed in the FBI's files, it is a fact that Corso was an investigator for Senator Richard Russell, who was on the Warren Commission that investigated the assassination of President Kennedy. It also transpires that Russell had a major UFO sighting while visiting Russia in 1955 that was subsequently investigated, extensively, by both the CIA and the Air Force. It is known, from cryptic comments that he made, that Russell received a classified briefing on the UFO subject from the CIA. Today, the agency claims it cannot locate the said briefing or any written, archived references to it. Interestingly, Russell was the one member of the Warren Commission who believed that a conspiracy lay behind President Kennedy's death.

At the time of his death in 1998, Corso was planning a follow-up book to *The Day after Roswell*. It had the working title of *The Day After Dallas* and would, so Corso claimed anyway, reveal the truth about the JFK assassination. But don't race to the Vault to check out the records on the controversial colonel. For reasons best known to officialdom, after taking down the Corso file from its old site, the FBI chose not to upload it to the Vault.

A CHASE FOR THE CIA'S SECRETS ON ROSWELL

Finally, there is the controversy-filled story of a man named Chase Brandon. He had a lengthy, and verifiable, career with the CIA, specifically in its Clandestine Service, the work of which involved covert operations, counterinsurgency-based projects, and weapons smuggling programs. He was also the CIA's entertainment liaison officer, which means he represented the CIA's interests in Hollywood, such as trying to ensure that the agency was presented in a good light by tinsel town's movie-makers. Brandon, in 2012, went public with an extraordinary story that, if true, suggested his bosses at Langley, Virginia, were sitting tight on the truth of what happened on the Foster Ranch in 1947.

According to Brandon, on one occasion during his years with the CIA, he spent time in the vault-like Historical Intelligence Collection—located at the agency's headquarters—when his attention was drawn to one particular file box. Hardly surprising, because the box had one word on it: *Roswell*. Brandon has remained cagey regarding what he actually saw and read as he dug into the file container. He did, however, state that both records and photos were included. Brandon maintained he would say no more. Many UFO researchers—even some of those who believe aliens may well have met their deaths in the wilds of New Mexico all those years ago—are highly skeptical of Brandon's assertions. Kevin Randle, the author of a number of pro-UFO books on Roswell, summed up his views in three, direct words that allow no room for misinterpretation: "Crapola, I say" (Randle, 2012).

Remember that whatever happened back in July 1947 did not actually occur in Roswell. It didn't even occur in Chaves County, which is the home of Roswell. Rather, it occurred on farmland in Lincoln County. Today, the journey to the site from the old Roswell Army Air Field takes about one and a half hours. Back then, when the roads and the vehicles were certainly not what they are today, the trip would have taken even longer. As much as the people of Roswell might not prefer to hear it, the *only* connection between the town itself and the legendary crash is that the wreckage was taken to Roswell because it was home to the nearest major military base. It's only in more recent years that the event and Roswell, the locale, have become fused into one. There's no reason, however, why, decades ago, the name "Roswell" should have been applied to a CIA file on the affair, because the connection between town and crash was not brought into being until 1980, when a book, *The Roswell Incident*—penned by Charles Berlitz and William Moore—was published. That's to say, it was UFO researchers, not the government, that promoted the Roswell link to the event.

The CIA agrees with Kevin Randle, although its staff has not been as to the point as Randle. Jennifer Youngblood, of the CIA's Office of Public Affairs, has stated unequivocally, albeit tactfully, that CIA historians, following up on Brandon's controversial assertions, did not find anything that, in any fashion, substantiated anything he said about Roswell. Perhaps of some significance,

UFO investigator Robbie Graham noted that while the CIA "brushed aside" Brandon's words, they stopped short of "directly calling him a liar." Maybe the story was just a tall one, designed to titillate the UFO faithful. Or, perhaps, Brandon really did see such a file, and it, like so many of the records on Roswell of the type that the General Accounting Office went after in the 1990s and found unavailable, is now missing too (Alford, 2012).

There is one final point worth noting on the matter of the vanished files of Roswell. It's inconceivable to imagine that, if extraterrestrials really did meet their deaths at Roswell, there would not be files stored somewhere. And those files—if they include such items as autopsy reports of dead aliens, photos of the crash site itself, and analyses of the wrecked UFO and its attendant technology, and so on—must be voluminous. The four years' worth of official documentation from the Roswell Army Air Force that is also missing must surely amount to a massive body of material, too. That neither Congressman Steven Schiff nor the power and clout of the Government Accountability Office could open the doors behind which the Roswell files are hidden suggests one, almost inevitable, scenario: The documents are locked down so tightly, and as far away from official oversight and scrutiny as possible, that they're not just missing. For all intents and purposes, *they're gone.*

Much the same can be said for the records and papers on a classic UFO case from the UK that, in terms of magnitude, rivals Roswell in the cosmically conspiratorial stakes.

4: YOU CAN'T SEE THE
FILES FOR THE TREES

Between the nights of December 26 and 29, 1980, multiple, extraordinary UFO events occurred within Rendlesham Forest, Suffolk, England, that involved military personnel from the nearby Royal Air Force stations of Bentwaters and Woodbridge. Since that now-long-gone period, countless U.S. Air Force personnel, who were stationed in the area at the time, have spoken out regarding their knowledge of a small, triangular-shaped object that was seen maneuvering in the forest. Others described seeing in the dark woods almost ghostly, extraterrestrial-type beings of short size and with eerie, feline-like eyes. Strange and unknown lights were seen dancing around the night skies, circling both the forest and the twin military facilities. There were stories that the amazing movements of the UFOs were caught on radar. And there was even hushed talk of those military personnel involved in the incident being silenced by ominous Men in Black–style characters.

At least part of the incredible saga has been officially documented. It comes close to chillingly paralleling the final scenes in Steven Spielberg's 1977 movie, *Close Encounters of the Third Kind*. On January 13, 1981, Colonel Charles Halt of the U.S. Air Force, and a prime witness to a significant number of the curious events that took place in Rendlesham Forest, wrote a one-page memo to the British Ministry of Defense that outlined a wealth of extraordinary UFO-like activity in the area that spanned the course of several nights. In Halt's own words, which were born out of his personal recollections, "a red sun-like light was seen through the trees. It moved about and pulsed. At one point it appeared to throw off glowing particles and then broke into five separate white objects and then disappeared. Immediately thereafter, three star-like objects were noticed in the sky...the object to the south was visible for two or three hours and beamed down a stream of light from time to time" (Halt, 1981).

The affair—arrogantly and outrageously dismissed by the British government as being of no defense significance whatsoever, and likely due to the misidentification of nothing more than a nearby lighthouse—has been the subject of a significant number of books, intense media coverage, and even vigorous questioning within the highest echelons of officialdom. More than 30 years after the strange events occurred, they continue to provoke furious debate within the UFO research community. One of the reasons why that debate shows no sign of going away is that, just like with the Roswell incident of 1947, certain files on the affair—significant files, it should be stressed—appear to be missing.

PRISON PAPERS GET PURLOINED

One of the little-known rumors surrounding the Rendlesham Forest case is that, at the height of the strange encounters, a panicky British government was on the verge of evacuating a number of nearby prisons, all in the county of Suffolk, too. In the 1980s, the late Graham Birdsall, who was the editor of Britain's *UFO Magazine* from the 1990s to the early 2000s, had the opportunity to speak with George Wild—a prison officer at Armley Prison in the English city of Leeds—who had some intriguing data to impart on this notable aspect of the story. According to what Wild told Birdsall, a senior prison official from the British government's Home Office had once let it slip to him, Wild, that high-level orders had arrived at the nearby HM Prison Highpoint North advising staff to prepare for a possible evacuation of the inmates due to a matter of grave national security. The date was December 27, 1980. Well, if that *was* the case, wouldn't the prison governor's official log book for that period reveal and reflect the facts? Indeed, it might. That is, if we could find and study its potentially priceless pages.

The late Lord Hill-Norton, who served as chief of the British Defense Staff from 1971 to 1973, had a deep and personal interest in UFOs in general, and an even deeper one in Rendlesham specifically. On October 23, 1997, he officially raised in the government's House of Lords a question concerning the alleged, unusual activities at HM Prison Highpoint North, as outlined to Graham Birdsall by George Wild a decade earlier. The exchange, from the official record, reads thus: "Lord Hill-Norton asked Her Majesty's Government whether staff at Highpoint Prison in Suffolk received instructions to prepare for a possible

In 1980, UFOs invaded British airspace around RAF Bentwaters. ©Nick Redfern

evacuation of the prison at some time between 25 and 30 December 1980, and, if so why these instructions were issued" (Hill-Norton, 1997).

Lord Williams of Mostyn replied: "I regret to advise the noble Lord that I am unable to answer his question, as records for Highpoint Prison relating to the period concerned are no longer available. The governor's journal is the record in which a written note is made of significant events concerning the establishment on a daily basis. It has not proved possible to locate that journal" (Williams, 1997).

It was a man named Nick Pope, who investigated UFO reports for the Ministry of Defense from 1991 to 1994, who provided me with a printed copy of the above exchange. And although Pope did not subscribe to the idea that the British government was engaged in a Top Secret operation to hide the truth about the Rendlesham affair, even he admitted to finding it hard to accept that such an important piece of data as the governor's journal could simply vanish into oblivion without a trace.

One other thing on this highly curious aspect of the Rendlesham conspiracy: HM Prison Highpoint North is located in the Suffolk village of Stradishall, which is around 50 miles from Rendlesham Forest. Until 1970, a Royal Air Force airfield existed in the village, called, unsurprisingly, RAF Stradishall.

After the closure of the installation, the grounds were transformed into the prison. Notably, several select portions of the old airfield still fall under the jurisdiction of the Ministry of Defense. To this day, they remain strictly out of bounds to the general public, and that even extends to those who call the village of Stradishall their home.

And the story is far from over.

CLEARING OUT THE COLONY

Georgina Bruni was a veritable Sherlock Holmes–type sleuth when it came to trying to penetrate the web of intense secrecy that surrounded, and that still surrounds, the Rendlesham case. During the course of her research, Bruni heard rumors of no less than two additional prisons that were said to have been primed for full evacuation as unexplained lights circled ominously and fantastically in the starlit skies over Bentwaters and Woodbridge. They were, specifically, Blundeston Prison—found between the Suffolk towns of Lowestoft and Great Yarmouth—and Hollesley Bay Youth Correctional Center, which is only around eight miles from Woodbridge and known by local village folk as the Colony. On January 23, 2001, the ever-persistent Lord Hill-Norton brought up the matter of the Blundeston and Hollesley allegations in the House of Lords. He asked for clarification on claims, uncovered by Bruni, that staff at both locations received "instructions to prepare for a possible evacuation at some time between 25 and 30 December 1980" (Hill-Norton, 2001).

On the same day, the parliamentary under-secretary of state for the Home Office, Lord Bassam of Brighton, replied in just about the briefest of all brief replies possible: "We can find no record of any such instructions" (Bassam, 2002).

The British government never stated outright that the story told to Graham Birdsall by George Wild was bogus. Nor did the government claim that Georgina Bruni's sources were liars or fantasists. Rather, government officials admitted—grudgingly, one strongly suspects—that the official day-to-day journal from HM Prison Highpoint North was curiously missing, and that as far as the stories involving Blundeston and the Colony were concerned, no records could be found to validate or deny the stories. Admitting that "we can find no record of any such instructions" is a far cry from saying with 100 percent certainty that such instructions *never* existed. After all, Lord Hill-Norton's questions were posed more than 20 years after the events in Rendlesham Forest occurred, which was more than ample time for the relevant papers to go on a suspicious and convenient walkabout (Ibid.).

GOING VIRAL

In a July 31, 1994 lecture at Leeds, England, Charles Halt (formerly Colonel Charles Halt, USAF, and one of those who witnessed the strange object in Rendlesham Forest) divulged his recollections of what had occurred then almost 14 years previously. During the course of his lecture, Halt astounded the audience by revealing something that had been hitherto unknown. An unscheduled C141 transporter aircraft arrived at Woodbridge just hours after the initial encounter on December 26, 1980, and a group of what Halt notably described as "special individuals" departed from the aircraft, headed straight out of Woodbridge's East Gate, and disappeared into the forest. There are rumors that the group in question was out there to deal with something hazardous, possibly biological, and viral. It's time to take a look at a distinctly secret locale from where that group of special individuals likely originated (Halt, 1981).

Beyond any shadow of doubt, one of the most secretive of all government-connected installations situated within the confines of the United Kingdom is Porton Down, which calls the green and pleasant county of Wiltshire its home. Its overwhelmingly classified work focuses to a significant degree on exotic viruses and biological warfare. If a real-life zombie apocalypse ever occurs, none should be surprised if it breaks out at Porton Down.

Although work at Porton Down originally, and secretly, began at the height of the tumultuous First World War, it was not until the dawning of the 1940s that the installation became the central hub for British interest in, and concerns relative to, the expanding realms of chemical and biological warfare. From 1946 onward, one year after the successful defeat of Nazi Germany, Porton Down's work began to focus more on the defensive—rather than chiefly offensive—aspects of such issues, and in 1957 the installation was duly christened the Microbiological Research Establishment (MRE).

By the late 1970s, a decision was made to place the MRE under the control of a civil body. As a result, significant reorganization duly occurred: On April 1, 1979, the MRE became the Center for Applied Microbiology and Research. Then, in 1995, it was absorbed into the Defense Evaluation and Research Agency. Six years later, there was yet another change. DERA split into two organizations: a private body called QinetiQ, and the Defense Science and Technology Laboratory, a body steeped in official secrecy, as a result of the fact that it is an arm of the Ministry of Defense. Today, the facility is known as DSTL, Porton Down.

DEPARTMENT OF THE AIR FORCE
HEADQUARTERS 81ST COMBAT SUPPORT GROUP (USAFE)
APO NEW YORK 09755

REPLY TO
ATTN OF.   CD   13 Jan 81

SUBJECT: Unexplained Lights

TO: RAF/CC

1. Early in the morning of 27 Dec 80 (approximately 0300L), two USAF security police patrolmen saw unusual lights outside the back gate at RAF Woodbridge. Thinking an aircraft might have crashed or been forced down, they called for permission to go outside the gate to investigate. The on-duty flight chief responded and allowed three patrolmen to proceed on foot. The individuals reported seeing a strange glowing object in the forest. The object was described as being metalic in appearance and triangular in shape, approximately two to three meters across the base and approximately two meters high. It illuminated the entire forest with a white light. The object itself had a pulsing red light on top and a bank(s) of blue lights underneath. The object was hovering or on legs. As the patrolmen approached the object, it maneuvered through the trees and disappeared. At this time the animals on a nearby farm went into a frenzy. The object was briefly sighted approximately an hour later near the back gate.

2. The next day, three depressions 1 1/2" deep and 7" in diameter were found where the object had been sighted on the ground. The following night (29 Dec 80) the area was checked for radiation. Beta/gamma readings of 0.1 milliroentgens were recorded with peak readings in the three depressions and near the center of the triangle formed by the depressions. A nearby tree had moderate (.05-.07) readings on the side of the tree toward the depressions.

3. Later in the night a red sun-like light was seen through the trees. It moved about and pulsed. At one point it appeared to throw off glowing particles and then broke into five separate white objects and then disappeared. Immediately thereafter, three star-like objects were noticed in the sky, two objects to the north and one to the south, all of which were about 10° off the horizon. The objects moved rapidly in sharp angular movements and displayed red, green and blue lights. The objects to the north appeared to be elliptical through an 8-12 power lens. They then turned to full circles. The objects to the north remained in the sky for an hour or more. The object to the south was visible for two or three hours and beamed down a stream of light from time to time. Numerous individuals, including the undersigned, witnessed the activities in paragraphs 2 and 3.

CHARLES I. HALT, Lt Col, USAF
Deputy Base Commander

Colonel Charles Halt's memo on a UFO landing in Rendlesham Forest, England, in 1980.
©U.S. Airforce, 1981

A FOREST OF SECRETS

Georgina Bruni uncovered a fascinating story that may explain who the special individuals referred to by Colonel Charles Halt really were. Once again, it's a saga filled with files that can't be found. Shortly after the events at Rendlesham Forest took place, Bruni learned, a number of personnel from Porton Down were reportedly dispatched to the area amid a great deal of secrecy. Dressed in full-body protection suits, they entered the woods—for reasons that remain officially unknown. Prior to her death in 2008, Bruni confided in me the name of her source for the account; it was a respected individual who had spent a great deal of time studying the history of biological warfare. And Bruni's source was indeed a prime candidate to comment on matters relative to the secret work of staff at Porton Down: She wrote an acclaimed book on the matter of bio-warfare.

On January 11, 2001, Lord Hill-Norton, refusing to give up the fight for the truth, tabled questions at an official level with British authorities in an attempt to resolve the issue of the Porton Down allegations as they related to the Rendlesham case. He specifically wanted to know whether personnel from Porton Down had visited Rendlesham Forest in December 1980 or January 1981, and whether any tests had been carried out in either of those two areas "aimed at assessing any nuclear, biological or chemical hazard" (Hill-Norton, 2001).

Predictably, the response to Hill-Norton's questions, which came from Baroness Symons of Vernham Dean, was one with which, by now, we should all be familiar: "The staff at the Defense Evaluation and Research Agency (DERA) Chemical and Biological Defense (CBD) laboratories at Porton Down have made a thorough search of their archives and have found no record of any such visits" (Symons, 2001).

Just as is the case with the matter of HM Prison Highpoint North, Blundeston Prison, and the Hollesley Bay Youth Correctional Center, this carefully worded statement does not state that such records did not exist—only that the specific personnel who made the search were unable to locate anything relevant. Officialdom is *extremely* good at providing such carefully couched, and potentially misleading, replies. As a result, the controversy surrounding the seldom-discussed Porton Down-Rendlesham issue continues to languish in a domain dominated by obscurity, obfuscation, and brick walls.

DESTROYING THE EVIDENCE

Lord Hill-Norton was also fascinated by the possibility that the many and varied UFOs seen in the vicinity of Rendlesham Forest, between December

26 and 29, 1980, had been tracked on radar. So, he went looking for proof. In January 2001, when he attempted to get to the bottom of the matter of Porton Down's involvement in the Rendlesham case, Hill-Norton also asked the government whether it was aware of any "uncorrelated targets tracked on radar" at the time of the encounters, and whether it would be willing to "give details of any such incidents" (Hill-Norton, 2001).

It was up to Baroness Symons of Vernham Dean to give a reply that surely surprises no one: "Records dating from 1980 no longer exist. Paper records are retained for a period of three years before being destroyed. Recordings of radar data are retained for a period of thirty days prior to re-use of the recording medium" (Symons, 2001).

It was this reply that prompted Georgina Bruni to note: "It is a fact that radar tracking tapes are re-used but there should be paper records. If this is the case then why was researcher Nick Redfern able to get verbatim data (from the logs) in 1989?" Bruni's question was an important one. While making my own inquiries into Rendlesham in the 1980s, I had the opportunity to have a personal exchange with Squadron Leader E.E. Webster of Royal Air Force Eastern Radar Watton, itself situated hardly a million miles away from Rendlesham Forest. On January 16, 1989, Squadron Leader Webster informed me that while military regulations forbade him from making available to me photocopies of the base's log books, he could provide me with a verbatim quote from the one part of the relevant log that referred to the Rendlesham events. It confirmed that at 3:25 a.m. on December 28, 1980, staff at RAF Bentwaters had contacted personnel at Watton to inquire about any unusual aircraft activity in the area (Bruni, 2001).

Obviously, for Squadron Leader Webster to be able to quote—verbatim, no less—from the December 1980 records, is evidence they still existed when I was in contact with him in 1989. So, when Baroness Symons of Vernham Dean assured Lord Hill-Norton that "paper records are retained for a period of three years before being destroyed," she clearly didn't know what she was talking about. That or she chose to stubbornly stonewall (Symons, 2001).

ERADICATING THE OFFICIAL RECORD

Now we come to the most recent revelation on the mysterious matter of the missing files of Rendlesham. In May 2011, as the Freedom of Information Act revealed, 11 years earlier the British Ministry of Defense received a request from a member of the public for copies of its own records on the incident. In dealing with the request, government officials discovered what they termed a "huge" gaping hole where there should have been stacks of papers of a specifically defense-intelligence nature. The hunt was soon on to find out where those papers had gone. It was a quest that led one official to speculate that perhaps someone with access to the Rendlesham files had "taken them home." A far more intriguing document notes that the disappearance of certain files on Rendlesham—the specific contents of which remain unknown to this day—might be interpreted to mean that "a deliberate attempt had been made to eradicate the records covering this incident" (Henderson, 2011). Of that last possibility, I can only say: Finally, some common sense surfaces out of the mouth of government.

A UFO LOG BOOK VANISHES

Those of a skeptical mind might be inclined to conclude that all of the above amounts to nothing more than bureaucratic bungling when it comes to the UFO-related files on the Rendlesham Forest incidents of December 1980 that have seemingly vanished into the ether. The problem with this scenario is that it's not the first time it has happened in Britain. Nor was it, by any stretch of the imagination, the last. On the night of August 13, 1956, multiple UFOs penetrated the airspace of Suffolk, the same English county in which the Rendlesham Forest event occurred 24 years later. Strange and unidentified lights, giving every appearance of being under intelligent control, soared across the star-filled skies. Military aircraft were scrambled to try and intercept the unknown objects. The UFOs ran rings around the finest pilots of the Royal Air Force. Radar operators talked of certain, unknown aerial targets traveling at speeds close to 4,000 mph. Other radar personnel spoke of tracking UFOs that instantaneously accelerated to speeds of approximately 600 mph from hovering positions. In other words, it was a decidedly memorable night in usually sleepy old England.

Today, we know that at least several of the aircraft involved in the interception of the UFOs were dispatched from a military base called RAF Neatishead. The chief controller who gave the order to scramble was Squadron Leader Freddie Wimbledon, who I had the good fortune to interview in 1994. Wimbledon informed me that not only was his entire team—himself, a fighter-controller, a tracker, a corporal, and a height-reader—interrogated about the affair by a senior officer who had traveled from the Air Ministry in London, but that the relevant log book detailing the night's encounters was removed from Neatishead and taken to London. Wimbledon added to me, in carefully chosen words, that anyone who may have found themselves in such a situation would have to think carefully about speaking out publicly, since the specter of prosecution under the terms of the Official Secrets Act would always loom large (Redfern, 1994).

CAPTURED ON FILM, BUT MISSING FROM THE ARCHIVES

Ralph Noyes retired from the British Ministry of Defense in 1977 in the position of under-secretary of state. Eight years after his retirement, Noyes wrote a thought-provoking and entertaining novel on the Rendlesham Forest affair titled *A Secret Property*. Part-Robert Ludlum, part-John le Carre, and part-*X-Files*, Noyes's story was a dynamic one, filled with secret government projects, conspiratorial characters, and, at the heart of it all, a genuinely mystifying, but utterly real, UFO phenomenon. It was a book that many UFO researchers speculated told the truth of Rendlesham, but that was presented by Noyes in a fictional fashion to ensure that he was not prosecuted under the terms of the Official Secrets Act.

Noyes, also after his retirement, went on record as stating that one of the pilots involved in the August 1956 dogfight succeeded in shooting what is known as gun-camera footage of at least one UFO. Noyes added that he had occasion to view the film in question at the Ministry of Defense in Whitehall, London, at some point in 1970. Also in attendance, said Noyes, were a representative of the Meteorological Office, the director of Air Defense, and various personnel from the Air Staff. While the footage showed little more than blurry, moving lights in the night sky, the important thing is that it showed *something*. You might think that film of this caliber—showing a UFO in British airspace and filmed by an experienced military pilot—would be carefully preserved for posterity. Not according to the Ministry of Defense, it wasn't. It's another example of something that should exist, somewhere, but that had defied all attempts to uncover it. So we are earnestly told, anyway.

In 1994, I approached Nick Pope, the aforementioned UFO investigator for the Ministry of Defense, and asked him if he was willing to initiate a search for this priceless film. To Pope's lasting credit, he *was* willing. And he *did* make a search. The problem, however, is that the investigation came up blank and empty-handed. Pope told me, after the quest for the footage was over: "I liaised with our archive people, who are the sort of middlemen between ourselves and the Public Record Office [author's note: now called the National Archives]. They made a number of checks of any place where this material might have ended. No one is disputing that Ralph Noyes saw this footage and that it existed. That's not in dispute, as far as I'm concerned" (Redfern, 1994).

So what happened to the film? Where did it end up? Was it really, and incredibly, destroyed? Nick Pope had a few ideas of his own:

I suspect that one of two things happened. Either it got lost or destroyed somewhere because it wasn't seen as being of public interest at the time. Or, old footage deteriorates: it becomes unstable and you have to destroy it before it becomes a health and safety hazard. But I think Ralph himself said that the footage wasn't that spectacular. We did have a thorough look for it and unfortunately it didn't turn up. Given that we've now had a proper look, I think it's unlikely it will turn up. All I can say is we gave it our best shot (Ibid.).

Although I have no doubt that Nick Pope was speaking the truth regarding his personal role in this curious matter, I find it astonishing that such rare and, perhaps, unique footage would have been routinely destroyed. It would have been a relatively simple task, in 1970, when Noyes saw the film, to make duplicate copies, thus ensuring its survival for future study and reference. This becomes even more logical when one takes into consideration the defense aspects of the case. Here was an object, an apparent UFO, that flew skillfully through British airspace, that was tracked on radar, and that made good its escape from the finest British military interceptors of the day. Would the Air Ministry, and its successor, the Ministry of Defense, really have allowed incredible evidence pertaining to such an astounding event simply to disappear or face irreversible destruction? Most unlikely! Yet something along those lines is *exactly* what we are led to believe happened. Or did it?

A SECRET SAUCER STASH

Robin Cole is a UFO researcher based out of Cheltenham, England, who spent a great deal of the 1990s investigating the secret role played in UFO investigations by the Government Communications Headquarters, which, as noted earlier, is the British equivalent of the United States' National Security Agency. Cole has a brief story that might explain where at least some of this film footage seen by Ralph Noyes may once have resided. Cole says:

I gave a presentation for a small group of people here in Cheltenham in early 1997, and at the end of it this guy came up to me and said: 'I was very interested to hear what you had to say.' He continued that in 1958 he worked at a London address just off Waterloo called Hercules House. Basically, his job, which was in the Central Office of Information, was to ferry messages back and forth to various departments. On one occasion he was allowed to enter the vaults. Well, when he was down there, he noticed that there was a whole shelf of gun-camera footage and other film footage just labeled 'UFOs.' He's now retired, but he made it clear that he's still under the Official Secrets Act (Redfern, 1997).

While 1958 is certainly a long time ago, it is a fact that the Central Office of Information—which was born in 1946, out of the wartime, propaganda-spreading Ministry of Information—did operate from within Hercules House. It finally closed its doors in March 2012. As for that old footage, well, who knows where its current location might be? Perhaps it sits on a shelf in a vault marked Top Secret, closed to even the likes of Nick Pope when he went looking for answers to the riddle in the early 1990s.

GONE WITH THE WIND

Finally, there comes a near-farcical case that demonstrates that convenient disappearances of potentially important UFO data of the British government have continued until recent times. Maybe it's *still* occurring. In 2002, the Ministry of Defense received a request for information from Lord Hill-Norton on a UFO sighting that, for a change, had nothing to do with the Rendlesham Forest case. But it was equally fascinating, nevertheless. The report was made in Norwegian territory by the crew of the *HMS Manchester*, a British Royal Navy destroyer ship that saw action in the Gulf War of 1991. The story had come to Hill-Norton's attention thanks to one of the crew members who decided to confide in him, on the understanding that he would be granted anonymity. Hill-Norton told the MoD that his source had been able to pinpoint the date as either the latter part of 1998 or at some point in February 1999: "Apparently the ship encountered an unidentified craft during a naval exercise, with several hundred people on *Manchester* and other HMS ships witnessing the event. At the same time, personnel on a Norwegian naval ship tracked the object on radar and were openly discussing the incident on the Operations Rooms communications network" (Hill-Norton, 2002).

The papers that documented just about every aspect of *HMS Manchester's* activities in the final months of 1998 were found and duly and carefully examined. They showed no evidence of any UFO encounters having occurred at all. So what about February 1999? Well, that's an entirely different matter. Lord Bach, the parliamentary under-secretary of state for defense procurement, and the man who had the job of investigating the claims, replied to Lord Hill-Norton that the log book for the particular time period could not be found. It was the HM Prison Highpoint North saga all over again. Whereas no good reason was ever given for the loss of the governor's log from Highpoint, a very creative—even amusing—explanation was provided regarding why the *HM Manchester's* log for February 1999 could not be located: It had blown overboard. No, I'm really not making this up. Whether or not someone in the government was, however, is something else entirely.

Lord Bach said, in apparent total seriousness:

> *The log was positioned, as is the custom, at the head of the gangway when the vessel was alongside in port, and an unusually strong gust of wind carried it overboard. In light of the missing document, my officials have contacted the commanding officer of the Manchester at the time. He has stated nothing that could be remotely construed as an unusual event or sighting involving unidentified aerial craft occurred during this or any other of Manchester's deployments while he was in command (Bach, 2012).*

How curious and convenient that not just a *regular* gust of wind, but an *unusually strong* gust of wind, should have resulted in the loss of the same log that almost certainly contained crucial data on a UFO encounter of profound proportions. Whether it's the governor's journal from an English prison, film footage taken by Royal Air Force pilots, a ship's log book, a pile of defense-intelligence files, or secret records from Porton Down, they all have one thing in common, aside from UFOs: No one can find them.

CONTAMINATION AND NEAR-DESTRUCTION

Finally, on the matter of the British government's UFO files, we have a case that should have ended in large-scale destruction, but amazingly and thankfully, did not. Few people have so diligently sought out the truth surrounding the British government's involvement in the UFO controversy than Dr. David Clarke, a lecturer in journalism at England's Sheffield Hallam University. In 2007, while trying to chase down certain UFO files compiled by a secret defense-intelligence arm of the British Ministry of Defense called DI55, Clarke learned that the government was planning on destroying two dozen files that appeared to be relevant to his studies. The reason: contamination by deadly asbestos years earlier.

Also set to share a similar fate were a staggering 63,000 contaminated files on other defense-intelligence subjects that, collectively, ran to somewhere in the region of *12 million pages*. The MoD made one big blunder in this saga: namely, that of letting Clarke know about the contamination and the gigantic scale of the planned destruction of files. He quickly lobbied that instead of destroying the material, the government should take diligent steps to at least try to preserve it in some form other than the original, now-contaminated, paper. Faced with the awkward fact that they had revealed their cards to Clarke (no less than a journalist) about how they were about to destroy millions of pages of material, British authorities caved in. They agreed to launch a multi-million-pound program to have the pages scanned and saved electronically. How many other files, for myriad other reasons through the years, might not have been so lucky is hard to say. But when the Ministry of Defense casually plans to destroy around 12 million pages of material—and with barely a second thought in evidence—it's a safe bet this isn't the first time there has been a large-scale destruction of documents in the heart of the British intelligence community.

Rendlesham and Roswell aren't the only prominent examples of where UFO files of a classified nature have conveniently vanished into apparent nothingness. As will now become evident, they are just the beginning.

5: UFO DOSSIERS: DENIED AND DISAPPEARED

Born in 1897, Wilhelm Reich was an Austrian psychoanalyst who fled to New York in 1939, in part at least, to escape the growing threat posed by the Nazi regime of Adolf Hitler. It was while in New York that Reich began talking about his alleged discovery of a strange and eerie life force, a kind of primordial, cosmic energy that he came to believe was located all across the Universe and within every living thing. He termed it Orgone, or OR. Reich also claimed to have uncovered something he termed DOR, or Deadly Orgone Radiation. Having carefully studied both OR and DOR, Reich believed that Orgone was the power source of the many UFOs that were seen soaring across the skies of the United States from the late 1940s onward. And although some of the entities piloting the craft were benign, Reich said in warning tones, others were anything but.

In response to the hostile aliens in our midst, says Reich authority Kenn Thomas, Reich came up with an ingenious invention to try and combat them. It was dubbed the Cloudbuster. Kenn Thomas says of the Cloudbuster that it was "...a cannon mounted on the back of a truck that concentrated and redirected orgone, which was aimed and fired at the UFOs, causing them to disappear." Thomas adds of Reich: "In the following years, he brought these devices with him to Tucson, Arizona," where he "did battle" with flying saucers (Thomas, 2011).

Interestingly, Reich had a Roswell connection. On one occasion in 1955, when he was journeying to Tucson, Reich decided to make an overnight stop in Ruidoso, New Mexico. To do so meant first passing through Roswell. In his own *Contact With Space*, Reich wrote of what happened as Roswell loomed large on the horizon: "Although it was very hot as we neared Roswell, New Mexico, no OR flow was visible on the road, which should have been shimmering with 'heatwaves.' Instead, DOR." In other words, malevolent UFOs were in the area. How curious, because in 1955 the Roswell link to UFOs was not on anyone's radar—the events of 1947 having long been forgotten by those who got briefly excited by the press release suggesting a UFO had crashed on the Foster Ranch. It was not until the mid-to-late 1970s that two UFO researchers, Stanton Friedman and Bill Moore, began the job of reopening that particularly conspiratorial can of worms (Reich, 1957).

DEATH, DECLASSIFICATION, AND DISAPPEARANCE

In 2000, the FBI declassified almost 800 pages of documentation on Wilhelm Reich. The Bureau's thoughts on the man can be summed up from the following words, which are contained in one particular FBI report:

> *This German immigrant described himself as the Associate Professor of Medical Psychology, Director of the Orgone Institute, President and research physician of the Wilhelm Reich Foundation and discoverer of biological or life energy. A 1940 security investigation was begun to determine the extent of Reich's communist commitments. A board of Alien Enemy Hearing judged that Dr. Reich was not a threat to the security of the U.S. In 1947, a security investigation concluded that neither the Orgone Project nor any of its staff were engaged in subversive activities or were in violation of any statute within the jurisdiction of the FBI ("FBI Adds New Subjects to Electronic Reading Room," 2000).*

Nevertheless, the FBI continued to keep a watchful eye on Reich until 1956, when tragedy struck, as researcher Greg Bishop—who has studied the life and career of Reich closely—notes: "Wilhelm Reich was jailed and tried for his refusal to appear in court on interstate commerce and fraud charges, and by court injunction many of his books were burned in an incinerator in lower Manhattan in 1956." He died in the Lewisburg Federal Penitentiary, Pennsylvania, on November 3, 1957, proclaiming to the bitter end that he had been set up by the government to take a fall for his many and varied discoveries, and still firmly believing in the existence of Orgone-powered UFOs of both a benign and hostile nature (Bishop, 2000).

The FBI's 789-page file on Wilhelm Reich went online at the Bureau's original Website back in 1999. It remained there until 2007 when, without any warning or word of explanation, it was removed. On top of that, despite its extensive length and its subject—the life and career of a man of historical note and controversy—the file has never been posted to the Vault, even though it could be found at the original site for almost eight years. The FBI has an explanation for this. When it became clear that the file on Reich was gone from the FBI's Website, questions were asked by a supporter of the Wilhelm Reich Infant Trust, a body based in Rangeley, Maine. Its activities involve running the Wilhelm Reich Museum, taking careful care of Reich's decades-old archives, and publishing new editions of his old and hard-to-find books and papers. That supporter, who questioned the FBI, was a philosophy professor, Philip Bennett, PhD. The FBI told Bennett:

> *The answer to your question was received from our Records Management Division (RMD) but we thought they were going to notify you. It was our mistake and I am sorry for the delay this has caused. Wilhelm Reich's file was intentionally taken off the Electronic Reading Room. Last year, RMD worked closely with the FBI's Historian to identify files which were either historically valuable or were popular files, that is more than 3-4 requests in the past 3 years. The file in question didn't make the list, so they removed it from the website* ("September 2008 Update from the Wilhelm Reich Infant Trust & the Wilhelm Reich Museum," 2008).

That's all well and good, because the FBI certainly *did* have a directive in the 2000s to remove from its original site those records perceived as not being of particular historical importance, or of dwindling interest to the public. Yet, on this same matter, staff at the Vault state they have now reinstated those "dozens of records previously posted" that had originally been "removed as requests diminished" (Ibid.). So why is it that those "dozens of records" specifically *don't* include the missing records on Wilhelm Reich?

This in itself is most odd, because the FBI has added to the Vault a number of other significant UFO-themed files, such as (a) a whopping 1,700-page collection of UFO data covering 1947 to 1977; (b) more than 120 pages of documents on New Mexico–based cattle mutilations that occurred in the mid-to late-1970s; (c) various papers on the Air Force's UFO study program, Project Blue Book; (d) a folder on Silas Newton, a controversial character who claimed knowledge of crashed UFO incidents in 1940s-era New Mexico, and who was a major informant in Frank Scully's 1950s hit book, *Behind the Flying Saucers*; and (e) a handful of papers that refer to the Roswell affair, but which shed no meaningful light on what did or did not happen back in the summer of 1947.

The Vault is an important and extensive resource tool for historians, journalists, authors, researchers, and members of the public. And it provides an incredible amount of formerly classified documents on numerous, diverse topics that throws much welcome light on American history. But, just like all vaults, this one is not without its secrets.

SOMETHING CRASHES AND FILES VANISH

On the afternoon of December 9, 1965, something strange plummeted to earth in an area of dense woodland close to the town of Kecksburg, Pennsylvania, some 30 miles south east of the city of Pittsburgh. The number of witnesses to the descent of the object was immense: It was seen crossing the skies of several U.S. states and entire swathes of southernmost Canada. Emergency lines were jammed and the media was soon onto the story. In the immediate aftermath of the crash, there was hushed talk in town of the military quickly cordoning off the woods, of a strange object—acorn-like in shape—having been recovered, and of pulverized, non-human bodies found strewn around the crash site. Was this a Pennsylvanian equivalent of the notorious Roswell, New Mexico, event of then almost two decades earlier?

Even within the UFO research field there is dissent in the ranks, and a great deal of division regarding the nature of the craft that came down at Kecksburg. Some investigators believe that a vehicle from a faraway world really did slam into the heart of those Pennsylvania woods back in 1965. Others, meanwhile, suggest that maybe the object was a satellite, one built by either the Soviet Union or the United States. Of course, if a Soviet spacecraft did fall into the hands of the United States, then the matter would indeed have been treated with overwhelming secrecy. Arguably, such secrecy would have rivaled that relative to a genuine, recovered UFO. After all, it's not every day that one has a state-of-the-art Soviet spacecraft fall into one's lap.

Interestingly enough—and serving to confuse the matter even more—a Soviet satellite actually *did* plummet to earth on that same day. Its name was Cosmos 96. And guess what? It was distinctly acorn-shaped, just like the device seen at Kecksburg. The problem, however, is that the crash site of Cosmos 96 was nowhere near Pennsylvania. Rather, Cosmos 96 disintegrated over Canada, several hours *before* the Kecksburg incident even occurred. Nevertheless, the odd coincidence (if that is what it was, and nothing else) of something unknown hurtling towards Earth at Kecksburg on the same day as Cosmos 96, coupled with the fact that both objects were of a similar design, has led many

UFO students to believe that something deeply profound occurred in the skies of the United States on December 9, 1965.

Did a UFO play a role in bringing down Cosmos 96? Might an alien spacecraft have malfunctioned and crashed after secretly tracking the spiraling movements of the decaying Russian craft? Or, was Cosmos 96 not the only Soviet space vehicle that came to grief that day? Did, incredibly, *another* Soviet craft come down, at Kecksburg, only hours after Cosmos 96 disintegrated? And, if so, was it secretly retrieved by elements of the U.S. military? Leslie Kean, a well-respected UFO researcher who has taken a deep interest in the Kecksburg affair, went looking for all the answers. She also wanted the definitive files on the Kecksburg case. Ultimately, and sadly predictably, she got neither.

On March 27, 2007, Emmet G. Sullivan, a United States District Judge for the District of Columbia, signed off on a suit against the National Aeronautics and Space Administration (NASA), which Leslie Kean herself had initiated. Kean, the Director of Investigations of the Coalition for Freedom of Information, was determined to force the space agency to release all of its files on Kecksburg. That's to say, documents, analyses of the recovered object, photographs of the crash site—everything. Because NASA had a wealth of material on file regarding the orbital decay and ultimate crash of Cosmos 96 on the same day, it seemed a safe and logical bet that NASA would have also been monitoring the movements of whatever it was that attracted so much intrigue and secrecy at Kecksburg. Well—surprise, surprise—that seems not to have been so.

The suit was packed with legal talk, much of a mind-numbing and bureaucratic nature. It did, however, note two things that surfaced during the course of Kean's quest for the truth. First, NASA had made blatant, contradictory assertions concerning its records—or rather, as NASA asserted, its *lack* of records—on Kecksburg. Second, Kean noted what she perceived was a lack of apparent dedication on the part of NASA when it came to actually looking for the files in the first place. None of it did any good, however. If voluminous files on Kecksburg were being hidden by NASA, they stayed hidden—lawsuit or no lawsuit. In the final months of 2009, Kean revealed the latest news in this curious set of circumstances. It was focused on (a) NASA's oddly missing documentation on Kecksburg and (b) the issue of records that, in error or by design, NASA had possibly shredded. Kean had to admit, when summing up where things were at as of late 2009: "Without additional, very extensive work, we'll never know the answers, and even with the work, we still might never know" (Kean, 2009).

Today, the Kecksburg files have still yet to surface. The mystery of what it was that came down in that certain stretch of Pennsylvanian woods on December 9, 1965, remains exactly that: a mystery.

A UFO OVER IRAN AND A ONE AND A HALF INCH THICK FILE

Strange and amazing things were afoot in the night skies of Tehran, the capital of Iran, on September 19, 1976. Those things revolved around the pilot of the Iranian Air Force practically going to war with a potentially hostile unidentified flying object. Not surprisingly, a U.S. government file was created on the event. Even less surprising, most of that file has vanished as mysteriously as did the UFO itself, all those years ago. For at least some insight into what happened on September 19, 1976, we are reliant upon one of just two pieces of evidence that *have* surfaced, via the Freedom of Information Act. The first is a three-page paper titled *Now You See It, Now You Don't!* It was penned by Captain Henry S. Shields of the U.S. Air Force. The second is a three-page document from the Defense Intelligence Agency. The latter reads like science-fiction. Astonishingly, it is nothing of the sort.

According to the paperwork at issue, it was not long after midnight on the 19th when people living in the Shemiran area of Tehran reported seeing strange, unidentified lights maneuvering directly overhead. Phone calls were quickly placed with local police and military authorities at Shahrokhi Air Force base. An hour or so after the first call reached staff at the air base, a McDonnell Douglas F-4 Phantom aircraft was scrambled to determine the precise origin of the enigmatic lights. And that's when things got interesting, as the following, extracted from the Defense Intelligence Agency's report, reveals:

> *At 0130 hrs on the 19th the F-4 took off and proceeded to a point about 40 NM north of Tehran. Due to its brilliance, the object was easily visible from 70 miles away. As the F-4 approached a range of 25 NM, [the pilot] lost all instrumentation and communications...When the F-4 turned away from the object and apparently was no longer a threat to it, the aircraft regained all instrumentation and communications (Defense Intelligence Agency, 1976).*

Notably, the documentation adds: "The size of the radar return was comparable to that of a 707 tanker," which would have put its length in excess of 140 feet and its width more than 130 feet (Ibid.).

Despite the brief malfunctions to his aircraft, the pilot was not dissuaded by the actions of this unearthly, and uninvited, visitor. He diligently headed off in hot pursuit. That's when a chase became an aerial dogfight. According to the DIA: "The object and the pursuing F-4 continued on a course to the south of Tehran when another brightly lighted object, estimated to be one-half to one-third the apparent size of the moon, came out of the object" (Ibid.).

This smaller UFO didn't just exit its mother-ship: It headed straight for the F-4 at violent, breakneck speed. The pilot, reacting quickly in the face of something unknown, "...attempted to fire an AIM-9 missile at the object but at that instant his weapons control panel went off and he lost all communication." Seconds later, noted the DIA, the two UFOs joined as one and shot away—not into the night sky, as you might imagine, however, but toward the ground. There was no crash, though, which is what the pilot was anticipating. Rather, the pilot of the F-4 reported that, even at an altitude of 15,000 feet, he could see the object illuminating the desert floor, seemingly having made a perfect touchdown. Aliens, quite possibly, had just landed in Iran. Given that the territory below was pitch black, the on-site investigation did not begin until the following morning, when the pilot was flown by helicopter to the area where the UFO had landed, which happened to be a dry lake bed. The Iranian military investigators who were also brought to the site concluded that, whatever the true nature of the UFO, it was now long gone (Ibid.).

When one considers all of the aspects of this extraordinary case—such as the ability of the UFO to disable both the weapon- and communication-systems of the Phantom F-4—there's a good likelihood that a lengthy file was prepared on the matter by U.S. Intelligence. Back in the 1970s, Iran and the United States were on far friendlier terms than they are in today's fraught world. From the 1960s to the 1970s, no less than 225 Phantom F-4s were sold to the Iranian Air Force by the U.S. government. It makes perfect sense that the Americans would have been disturbed by the ease with which one of their own aircraft was overwhelmingly prevented from taking decisive action against the UFO hurtling toward it. The U.S. military would surely have wanted to get to the bottom of who, or what, commanded such aircraft-disabling technology, right? Right! So, what does the military's file on the matter say about it all? Well, aside from the three pages of raw intelligence, from which the quotes above were word-for-word extracted, we have nada. That's not to say, however, that nada is all there is to find.

UFO researchers Barry Greenwood and Lawrence Fawcett spent a great deal of personal time and effort digging into the matter of the Iranian Air Force incident of September 1976. They noted that the Defense Intelligence Agency papers on the case specifically stated that "more information will be forwarded when it becomes available" (Defense Intelligence Agency, 1976).

Unfortunately, for those of us outside of officialdom at least, such has not yet happened. There are, however, good indications that a substantial file was created on the event and remains hidden from public view. In the words of Greenwood and Fawcett: "Reliable sources within the government have told us

In 1976, a McDonnell-Douglas Phantom aircraft engaged a UFO in an aerial dogfight over Iran. ©Nick Redfern

that the Iranian case file was about one and a half inches thick, yet absolutely no admission to having this file has come from any government agency with a possible connection to the case" (Fawcett and Greenwood, 1984).

And there ends the remarkable story. The words of Greenwood and Fawcett in relation to that huge file were made in 1984. Three decades later, there's still no sign of the documentation surfacing any time in the near future.

AUSTRALIA LOSES ITS UFO FILES

In one of those surreal situations in which truth really is stranger than the strangest of all fictions, in early June 2011, the Australian Department of Defense revealed to the world that it had "lost" its collection of UFO files. The revelation surfaced in the immediate wake of a two month-long quest to find the records. The search itself had been prompted by a Freedom of Information Act request, submitted by the *Sydney Morning Herald* newspaper, for Australia's UFO papers to be declassified. Only when senior military intelligence staff went looking to decide what could, and what could not, be declassified did they find that it didn't really matter after all, because there was nothing to declassify—at

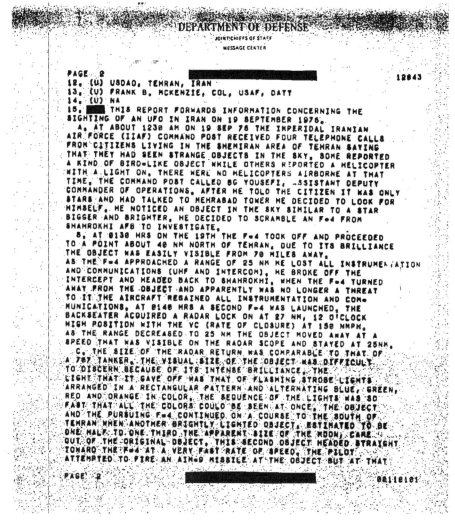

One of the very few documents to have surfaced on the Iranian UFO incident of 1976. ©U.S. Department of Defense, 1976

least, that is, aside from one solitary file titled *Report on UFOs/Strange Occurrences and Phenomena in Woomera* (Taylor, 2011).

Natalie Carpenter, of Australia's Freedom of Information Office, said that searches were undertaken at a variety of official establishments, including the Headquarters Air Command RAAF Base Glenbrook; the Canberra-based National Archives; and the Defense Record Management System. It was all to no avail: "...the files could not be located and Headquarters Air Command formally advised that this file is deemed lost" (Ibid.).

Because, officially, at least, the Australian Government had been out of the UFO game since 1996, it was seen as nothing but normal administrative procedure to destroy the files, Carpenter added. Curiously, however, it wasn't just the files that were missing; the surrounding documentation that gave the order for the files to be destroyed was gone, too.

Staff of the *Sydney Morning Herald* newspaper asked: "Could there be any better fodder for Australia's conspiracy theorists?" Almost certainly not! And it wasn't just the staff of the newspaper that decided to have their say on the matter (Besser, 2011).

Doug Moffatt, the spokesperson of a civilian group, UFO Research New South Wales, made a very good point in relation to this breaking news: "It would be interesting to know if they have thrown anything else out. If not, it starts looking dodgy." Indeed, it would look dodgy if the UFO files had been specifically selected for destruction, while other files, perhaps of a tedious, bureaucratic nature, had not ("Australia UFO Sighting Files Mysteriously Disappear," 2011).

Calling the loss of the files "chilling," UFO authority Whitley Strieber, one week after the story broke, had his say on the matter, too:

> *Last week, the Australian government announced that it has 'lost' its UFO files. Thus it joins the United States, which 'lost' all the files relating to the Roswell AFB dating from 1947 through 1952, and the United Kingdom, which recently announced that it has 'lost' all the files relating to the Rendlesham Forest UFO Case. Rendlesham and Roswell are the two most important UFO cases ever to have taken place. Australia is a UFO hotspot, and sightings are frequent in the area of the US's Pine Gap signals intelligence facility (Strieber, 2011).*

Strieber's point was an important one: Pine Gap is the Australian equivalent of the United States' National Security Agency. In fact, the governments of Australia and the United States control the facility in a 50-50 situation. It is absurd to imagine that files pertaining to frequent, unknown aerial activity in the skies over such a highly sensitive location as Pine Gap would be destroyed so casually (Strieber, 2011).

Even Nick Pope—the now-retired British Ministry of Defense man who tried, but ultimately failed, to find that priceless bit of film footage of a UFO in action over the UK in August 1956—chimed in with a comment or two on this controversial matter: "I can understand why UFOlogists and conspiracy theorists might react to the loss of files, particularly with the Australian story having come after the British story about the Rendlesham files. I can understand why people would say, 'This must be a conspiracy'" ("Australia UFO Sighting Files Mysteriously Disappear," 2011).

6: INVENTING AN ALIEN INVASION

Referenced in now-declassified Federal Bureau of Investigation memoranda of May 6, 1955, as an Evangelist preacher—and one who spent much of his time loudly warning anyone who would listen about the perils and threats posed by communism—Kenneth Goff was born in Wisconsin in 1914. For someone whose world was focused to a significant degree on matters of an evangelical nature and the communist way of life, it is intriguing to note that he also had complex and conspiratorial ties to the UFO issue.

Not only that, Goff was also the subject of a number of official files that remain classified, either in part or in whole, to this day, many years after his death. The declassified FBI files on Goff are significantly redacted. The CIA's papers on Goff are withheld, in total, for national security reasons. Though military intelligence files on the man exist, they have not yet seen the light of day. This is quite a revelation and an achievement for someone who spent most of his time working as a preacher.

A good indication of the nature of the matters that regularly occupied Kenneth Goff can be gained from noting the titles of some of his lectures. They included: *Treason in Our State Department*; *Should We Use the Atom Bomb?*; *Red Secret Plot for Seizure of Denver*; and *Do the Reds Plan to Come by Alaska?* Goff was also a prestigious author, one who published books by the shelf-load. *Will Russia Invade America?*; *One World, A Red World*; and *Confessions of Stalin's Agent* were just three of literally dozens of titles he churned out for his fans and followers.

IDENTIFYING A DOUBLE-AGENT

Given that Kenneth Goff, a seemingly patriotic American, was loudly warning about the perils of communism and the potential threat posed to the United States by the former Soviet Union, one would imagine that his vocal stance would have greatly pleased the FBI. Not at all. When the Bureau began to look into the world of Goff, its agents discovered that he had previously been a public supporter of communism. The redacted files on Goff make it clear that there were major concerns in the Bureau that Goff was *still* a communist, albeit a secret one whose goal was to try and infiltrate anti-communist groups in the United States. Goff's overall purpose, the FBI came to suspect, was to worm his way into the organizations and then secretly destroy them from within. The Bureau may have been on the right track when it came to suspicions about his potential Trojan Horse–style actions.

Of the few pages of official files that *have* surfaced on Goff, those that stand out refer to him as having been a fully paid-up member of the Communist Party during the late 1930s and throughout the early to mid-1940s. By the latter part of the 1940s, however, Goff's views on communism had radically changed. Or, perhaps, it's more correct to say that his views had radically changed *publicly*.

In early February 1948, Goff was arrested outside of the Washington, D.C.–based Soviet Embassy. The reason for Goff's arrest: He was seen positioning large placards—denouncing both communism and the Soviet way of life—against the embassy's perimeter. He also stopped people as they walked past the embassy, warning them of the threat the Russians posed to the Western world. Some of those people claimed that Goff's warnings bordered upon physical harassment, as he followed them up and down the street, ranting and raving as he saw fit. Police officers soon turned up on the scene and arrested Goff. On February 25th, he was fined $100 for causing a disturbance to the peace outside the embassy.

Three years later, Goff was still doing his best to present himself as a hater of communism. In October 1951, Goff was arrested and ended up in the Denver, Colorado, Municipal Court for tearing up a Soviet flag outside of Denver's Civic Center. The FBI, however, was still concerned that Goff's actions were not all that they initially seemed to be. Was he still up to his old, secret tricks of trying to identify pro-active anti-communists and then find ways to manipulate them and, ultimately, to nullify their actions? The Bureau clearly considered this to be a major possibility: "It has been our concern that Goff always ensures he is seen while displaying anti-Soviet tendencies. [Deleted] has remarked that if Goff is still privately 'of a party mind' this might explain his public displays" (Federal Bureau of Investigation, 1951).

FLYING SAUCERS, FLUORIDE, AND A FAKED ALIEN INVASION

As well as being a possible, but secret, Russian asset, Goff was also a full-on conspiracy theorist. In 1953, long before it was fashionable, Goff lectured on what he perceived to be the perils posed by fluoride. Indeed, one of his self-published and somewhat-obscure pamphlets dealt with what Goff claimed was a secret, fluoride-based program initiated by none other than the Kremlin. As Goff told it, Soviet agents—active within the heart of the United States itself—were clandestinely adding massive amounts of fluoride to America's water supply as a means to dumb down the entire population.

Goff came to believe, however, that the biggest conspiracy of all revolved around UFOs. As evidence of this, one of his most popular lectures, which packed the theaters wherever and whenever he spoke, went by the name of *Traitors in the Pulpit, or What's Behind the Flying Saucers—Are They From Russia, Another Planet, or God?* Whereas most UFO researchers in 1950s America believed that the flying saucer mystery was one of definitive extraterrestrial origins, Goff most certainly did not. It was his thought-provoking opinion that flying saucers were the secret, and highly advanced, creations of military agencies. In Goff's mind, one day this classified armada of craft would be unleashed upon the world, en masse, as a means to fool the Human Race into believing that we were faced with an alien threat, when in reality it was a threat from *within*.

The reason for such a ruse, Goff believed, was as downright incredible as it was sinister. In his own words:

> *During the past few years, the flying saucer scare has rapidly become one of the main issues, used by organizations working for a one-world government, to frighten people into the belief that we will need a super world government to cope with an invasion from another planet. Many means are being used to create a vast amount of imagination in the minds of the general public, concerning the possibilities of an invasion by strange creatures from Mars or Venus (Goff, 1959).*

Goff continued in a similar vein, commenting on a famous radio version of H.G. Wells' acclaimed novel *War of the Worlds*: "...a radio drama, put on by Orson Welles…caused panic in many of the larger cities of the East, and resulted in the death of several people. The Orson Welles program of invasion from Mars was used by the Communist Party as a test to find out how the people would react on instructions given out over the radio. It was an important part of the Communist rehearsal for the Revolution" (Ibid.).

It is one thing to believe that UFOs exist. It is quite another to take the stance that those same UFOs are actually built by nefarious human forces who will, one day, expose each and every one of us to a fake alien attack, as a means to invoke martial law and the unveiling of a terrible New World Order of proportions that not even George Orwell—of *1984* fame—could visualize. Yet, that's precisely what Goff came to fully accept. It's worth noting that Goff's comments on UFOs and a one world government began in 1951.

In fact there are two reasons why this is important: (a) 1951 marked the year in which most of the official files on Goff, to which we are today denied access, were created; and (b) 1951 was the year in which something very unusual, and definitively ufological, happened to Goff himself. Goff recorded the details in a series of letters sent to a flying saucer researcher named Leon Davidson, who also happened to believe that UFOs had human, rather than alien, origins.

A MYSTERY MAN CALLS ON GOFF

According to what Goff told Davidson, in August 1951, he received a strange visit in the middle of the night from what was purported to be a definitive extraterrestrial visitor. That same visitor proceeded to pump Goff's arm full of mind-expanding chemicals. But this was no dwarfish, black-eyed alien of the type so often reported in UFO encounters today. Rather, Goff's late night visitor was a smartly dressed, human-looking alien. Not only that, it was an alien that wished Goff to spread the word that communism was a very bad thing and that E.T. hated Reds.

Goff might have been an odd character, but he was certainly no fool. After the strange figure vanished and Goff finally regained all of his senses, he recognized it simply could not have been a coincidence that he—with a fairly significant background in matters of a red nature—should have been warned about the perils of communism. Coupled with his well-publicized fears about chemicals being introduced into the water supply to affect the mindset of the American populace, Goff, perhaps *very* astutely, came to believe something incredible. Goff concluded that he had been targeted by some governmental agency that had, at its heart, a program involving (a) the creation of fabricated UFO-themed events; (b) the use of drugs to instill altered states in the targeted individual; and (c) a bigger picture of widespread manipulation and control of the populace via hoaxed UFO events—hence his absolute obsession with the whole *War of the Worlds*/one world government issue.

If we had access to the 1951 files on Goff generated by both the CIA and military intelligence, we might be able to get a clearer picture on the real identity of Goff's enigmatic, midnight rambler. That the records are withheld under the terms of the BI portion of the Freedom of Information Act, however—which protects national security-based issues—effectively means we don't have a clue as to the identity of the secret agent who, all those decades ago, possibly took on a classified assignment to masquerade as an alien.

GOFF: THE SCIENTOLOGY CONNECTION

Four years later, Goff was watched for another reason: He became chummy with L. Ron Hubbard, of Scientology fame, an organization that is well known for having more than a few links to beliefs in extraterrestrial life. Officialdom was watching Hubbard closely during the time that he and Goff first met, and significant portions of Hubbard's FBI file are now in the public domain. The sections of the file that deal with Hubbard and Goff, though, remain behind closed doors. But what we do know still reveals a notable story connecting the two.

In 1955, the Church of Scientology published a booklet titled *Brain-Washing: A Synthesis of the Russian Textbook on Psychopolitics*. Supposedly, it was a summary of the work of one Lavrentiy Beria, a Soviet politician, marshal of the Soviet Union, and chief of the Soviet security and secret police apparatus (NKVD) under Joseph Stalin during the Second World War. It has been suggested that *Brain-Washing* was taken from a lengthy speech that Beria delivered in 1950 on the subject of how psychiatry could be utilized as a tool of social control. Not everyone, however, is quite so sure that Beria had anything to do with it.

L. Ron Hubbard, Jr., has stated that his father wrote every word of it. Even more interesting, the introduction to a version of *Brain-Washing* in the hands of Morris Kominsky—the author of *The Hoaxers: Plain Liars, Fancy Liars and Damned Liars*—was written by Kenneth Goff. Another version attributes the *entire* work to Goff, despite the fact that the document is filled with what is clearly evidence of Hubbard's own writing style. Clearly, then, Goff and Hubbard were somehow interconnected. Plus, that (a) the booklet referenced matters

Lavrentiy Beria ©Wikipedia

related to "social control," something that Goff believed the UFO issue could majorly influence; and (b) Scientology is heavily alien-influenced, shows that Hubbard and Goff had more than a few things in common.

If we had access to the denied official files on the connection between the two men, we might know how deeply those commonalities ran. Unfortunately, we don't. Kenneth Goff died in 1972 while still only in his early 60s, so he is certainly not in a position to help us out with the answers. Whether Goff was a communist-hater, or someone ingeniously masquerading as such, and whether he was someone who had uncovered the amazing and controversial truth about a plot involving UFOs to enslave us all, we'll probably never know. Or, more likely, we will never know until officialdom decides to share those files that, right now, no one wants us to see.

Now it's time to take a close look at the missing, secret files on the rich and famous—those celebrities, stars, and larger than life characters that are instantly recognizable to one and all—and that includes to the classified world of government.

PART 3: FILES ON
FAMOUS FACES

7: MARILYN, MOON DUST, AND A MISSING DIARY

At her birth on June 1, 1926, she was given the name of Norma Jean Mortenson. We all know her far better as Marilyn Monroe. She had a notable career in the wild world of Hollywood that spanned more than a decade and a half. It was a career filled with hit movies, behind-the-scenes turmoil, emotional ups and downs, and secret affairs with powerful men in the world of politics. And it all came to a crashing and irreversible end in August 1962 when the world's most famous blond died at the age of just 36. But let's backtrack a bit before we get to the heart of the story, which is focused on certain documents on the star gone AWOL.

Shortly after her 20th birthday, Monroe was given one of those offers that are extremely hard to refuse. And there was no reason why she should have refused it. It was a prestigious contract with Twentieth Century Fox. Norma Jean was quickly gone and in her place was Marilyn. *The Asphalt Jungle, Gentlemen Prefer Blondes, Clash by Night, Niagara, Bus Stop* and the hit comedy *Some Like it Hot*, in which she starred opposite Jack Lemmon and Tony Curtis, were among Monroe's most memorable performances. But, behind the scenes, there was nothing but drama and sadness. Marilyn suffered deeply from self-esteem issues, and had a character that was easily hurt. On the other side of the coin, Monroe was very learned, had an incredible memory, and carefully followed the arena of world politics. Sadly, to cope with the many downs she experienced, Marilyn became hooked on a dizzying number of mood-altering drugs. They were provided by a Dr. Ralph Greenson, a psychoanalyst who happily dished out pills by the bucket-load to some of the biggest stars in Hollywood.

High-profile marriages to the well-known leftist playwright Arthur Miller and to baseball hero Joe DiMaggio followed Monroe's rise to fame, as did affairs with President John F. Kennedy, and his brother, Bobby, the attorney general. If you're going to jump into a bed with the president of the United States of America and his little brother, don't be surprised if a swathe of government agencies takes careful note of your every move. That's exactly what happened to Marilyn Monroe. From the 1950s and up until her death in Brentwood, Los Angeles, on August 5, 1962—some say via her own hand and a deadly cocktail of pills, whereas others point the finger at agents of government—Monroe was placed under the scrutiny of many a classified microscope.

MOSCOW, MARILYN, AND MILLER

The FBI has officially declassified a significant number of documents on Marilyn Monroe that are now available for all to view at the Bureau's Website, the Vault. They make for intriguing reading and demonstrate how J. Edgar Hoover secretly kept the blond beauty in his sights for years. Chief among the reasons were the Kennedy connections, Monroe's marriage to Arthur Miller, and her interest in socialism and the Soviet way of life. But it's not so much the *declassified* files that we *have* been allowed to see which concerns us here. Rather it's the *classified* ones we *haven't* been permitted to view. It's time to turn our attention toward the secret domain of the CIA.

There are strong indications that the CIA possesses a wealth of material on the actress. The problem, however, is that unlike the FBI, the CIA flat out denies having even a single, solitary scrap of paper on the woman who had intimate relationships with a president and an attorney general—maybe at the same time, too, it's rumored. That act alone suggests Monroe would have been, to the CIA, what is known in today's age of terror as a person of interest. But no, says the agency. Not then, not now; in fact, not ever. The problem with this unswerving, stubborn stance is that we can prove the CIA (actually, the director of the agency) was the recipient of data on one of the hottest Hollywood stars of all time, even if the CIA prefers to claim otherwise.

The first real inkling of undeniable involvement in the life of Marilyn Monroe on the part of the CIA dates back to August 19, 1955. It was on that date that, in J. Edgar Hoover's eyes, the actress committed the ultimate sin of all sins: She requested a visa to visit Communist Russia. Never one to ignore anything of a Soviet nature, the FBI swung into action, and the frantic tapping of typewriters resonated around the walls of FBI headquarters, as Bureau agents sought to quickly ascertain and record the facts. Having done so, the FBI distributed the salient points to other, senior sources within the intelligence community, including Dennis A. Flinn, the Director of the Office of Security at the State Department, and William F. Tompkins, the assistant attorney general. The documentation was also marked for the attention of the director of the CIA at the time, Allen Dulles. He held the position of director from 1953 to 1961, after which he was booted out by JFK, partly as a result of the CIA's botched role in the Bay of Pigs fiasco.

The Soviets were keeping the matter of Monroe's application under consideration, according to the FBI. Three days later, the FBI issued a further document concerning Monroe's activities—which it *also* forwarded to CIA director Dulles—the contents of which are unfortunately, but nevertheless intriguingly, completely blacked out under provision B1 of the Freedom of Information Act. Notably, B1 is a piece of legislation that specifically covers national security issues. Ultimately, Monroe chose not to visit Russia, and this particular investigation fizzled out. But, regardless of what the CIA officially says loudly to the contrary (and maybe a tad too loudly), we do see further evidence that there simply must be files on the actress hidden somewhere at the CIA's Langley, Virginia, headquarters.

Making even more of a mockery out of the CIA's "no files" position on Marilyn Monroe, the FBI shared with agency personnel its records on her third husband, Arthur Miller. As with *Mrs.* Miller, the CIA maintains that it has no files on *Mr.* Miller either, yet this can only be considered highly unlikely. Miller, from 1966 to 1969, happened to be the International President of PEN International, a worldwide body of writers created in London, England, in the early 1920s. PEN worked hard to highlight the lives and works of those writers, authors, and poets who have been harassed, and even killed, for their research into, and forthright comments on, human rights abuses and government cover-ups. Not surprisingly, during the Cold War, the CIA tried hard to worm its way into the heart of PEN, with the goal of secretly manipulating it from the inside outward.

So, for the CIA to have had deep links to PEN—combined with Miller's leftist politics, that he had served as PEN's International President for three years, and that he had been married to Marilyn Monroe, who wanted to visit Russia—it is near-inconceivable to argue the Agency would not have taken more than a passing interest in Arthur Miller and created its own case file on the man and one on his famous wife, too. Once again, secret files that *should* exist apparently, we are assured time and again by officialdom, *don't*. And it looks like there are yet further CIA files on the actress that can't be found. One of them may well relate to a strange, sex-filled, mid-to-late 1950s escapade.

MARILYN GIVES IT UP TO A PRESIDENT (NO, NOT JFK)

While she was shooting *Bus Stop*, a movie made in 1956, Marilyn Monroe had occasion to meet Indonesian president Sukarno, who, like a lot of Javanese people, had only one name. His meant good karma. It was a name that, on one particularly memorable night, proved to be most apt. The date of the encounter was June 1, 1956, which just happened to be Marilyn's 30th birthday. It so transpired that President Sukarno, who was well known for being quite a hit with the ladies, was visiting Los Angeles at the time. The result was that paths crossed, as they are often wont to do. Paths did a great deal more than just merely cross, however. The actress quietly confided in a close friend of hers, Robert Slatzer—about whom more shortly—that she and Sukarno spent what is tactfully known as an evening together. It was during the presidential visit and while Marilyn was busily celebrating her milestone birthday. And it was a night that Sukarno never forgot. But it was not just Slatzer who got the lowdown on one of at least two presidents that bedded the Hollywood blond. The CIA heard about it, too. And they decided to act on it in an odd but enterprising fashion.

This was, remember, the height of the Cold War, and the CIA was hardly on good terms with Indonesia, because it was largely due to Sukarno's actions that the country had taken a major fork in the road toward dastardly communism. Thus, from around 1957 onward, and throughout much of the 1960s, the CIA engaged in all kinds of clandestine, 007-style operations to oust Sukarno from power, none of which ever worked. Nevertheless, Sukarno *was* finally kicked out, in 1967, by the People's Consultative Assembly of the Republic of Indonesia, which was the legislative branch of the Indonesian political body.

Keeping the Sukarno-Marilyn rendezvous solidly in mind, in the late 1950s the CIA came up with a definitively harebrained scheme to try to discredit Sukarno. The plan was to bait him with a blond (actually a hired prostitute) even hotter than Marilyn, and have the pair head for a hotel room for a bit of nighttime fun and frolics. The idea was to install hidden cameras in strategic locations in the room, and to film the entire event, Pamela Anderson and Tommy Lee–style, or Pamela Anderson and Bret Michaels–style. The next step was to quietly inform Sukarno that, unless he moved Indonesia away from communism, the film would be spread far and wide among the world's media, along with rumors that the blond was a foreign, hostile agent. The idea was

Marilyn Monroe: the Hollywood star secretly watched by the CIA and the FBI. ©U.S. Army 1954

hastily dropped, however, when word reached the CIA that Sukarno had gotten wind of the project and was quite excited by the idea of showing of his virility to the world in big-screen, celluloid form. Seeing that things could seriously backfire on them, the CIA's finest chose not to proceed with their plans of the pornographic kind. The story, though, wasn't over.

In 1958, having learned that Sukarno had a voracious appetite for beautiful girls, and knowing all too well of his 1956 liaison with a certain Hollywood honey, the CIA took a different approach. For a brief time, instead of trying to oust the president, the agency actually, and surprisingly, attempted to reason with him and explained why communism was a very bad thing. If Sukarno would only model his nation in a fashion befitting that of the Western world, maybe the CIA could give him a nice reward in return. You guessed it: another night with Marilyn, who had already been approached by the CIA, and who was apparently quite enthusiastic about the prospect of a repeat performance with the man with just one name. Something, however, went wrong. Whatever it was remains tantalizingly unknown. Joseph Smith, a former CIA career officer in Asia, and one of the few agents to ever speak out on the subject, said: "There was an attempt to get Sukarno together with Monroe. In mid 1958 I heard of a plan to get them in bed together. I remember someone from Washington coming through and talking about 'some crazy business with Marilyn Monroe that didn't work out right'" (Summers, 1983).

The CIA's response to the Monroe-Sukarno situation is that nothing can be found in its archives to validate the story. There was, however, even crazier CIA-connected business on the horizon for the legendary movie star. In the end, it got downright tragic and deadly.

MARILYN MONROE AND "THINGS FROM SPACE"

All of the documentation on the matter of government secrecy and Marilyn Monroe that appears at the FBI's Website, the Vault, is 100 percent authentic in nature. There is, however, one particular *unauthenticated* document (and attendant story) in the public domain that bears scrutiny, because it is focused on Monroe, missing papers, a vanished diary, government secrets, the CIA, the actress's relationships with both JFK and Robert Kennedy, and the U.S. government's acquisition of what are described in the document as certain "things from space." Not only that, the document was dated just two days before Monroe's August 5, 1962, death. The controversy, though, began 23 years later, in 1995.

Milo Speriglio was an investigative author, now dead, who wrote three books on Monroe's untimely end. They were: *The Marilyn Conspiracy*; *Marilyn Monroe: Murder Cover-Up*; and *Crypt 33: The Saga of Marilyn Monroe*. In early 1995, said Speriglio, he obtained the controversial document at issue from a California-based UFO researcher named Timothy Cooper, who claimed to have received it from a government insider he had been contacted by some years earlier. In a Los Angeles–based press conference, Speriglio told the media that the purported CIA document contained classified information on how President John F. Kennedy had guardedly informed Monroe that he had secret knowledge of the notorious crashed UFO incident at Roswell, New Mexico, in July 1947. For two months, Speriglio sat on the document, too amazed to do anything but file it away. Finally, however, he decided to do a bit of digging and placed it into the public domain—hence the press conference.

The document also detailed how the actress was threatening to go public with the truth about various government secrets the Kennedy brothers had tantalized her with, chiefly as a means to impress her and get her into bed. The tactics of JFK, and his brother Bobby, had worked spectacularly well. Things were now, however, looking to go spectacularly badly.

The bulk of the contents of the document are purportedly based around telephone conversations between a man named Howard Rothberg, who was the owner of a New York–based antique store, and Dorothy Kilgallen. The latter was a well-known celebrity gossip columnist and TV personality of the 1950s and 1960s, who was herself the subject of a once-secret, 167-page FBI file, and someone who knew Marilyn Monroe personally. In addition to that, Kilgallen was the last person to interview Jack Ruby. He was the Dallas, Texas, night club owner, and buddy to the local Mob, who shot and killed JFK's alleged assassin, Lee Harvey Oswald.

Speriglio explained the Rothberg-Kilgallen connection: Rothberg was friendly with many of the press photographers that regularly followed Monroe. As a result, Rothberg often got to hear intriguing gossip on the actress. He would then feed that same gossip to Dorothy Kilgallen. There was far more to it than that, however. Rothberg was also Kilgallen's personal interior decorator, which meant the two had plenty of alone time to secretly discuss the latest titillating scandal about Hollywood's most loved star of that era.

The document, which was stamped Top Secret and dated only two days before Monroe's death on August 5, 1962, provides a summary of the remarkable story. According to an overview at the top of the page, the entire content was taken from wiretap conversations secretly recorded by the CIA, some of which were between Kilgallen and Rothberg; others involved Monroe and Robert Kennedy. Indeed, that the document amounts to a summary, or a briefing paper, strongly suggests somewhere there should be other files that tell the *full* story. Do I really need to tell you, at this stage, that they have failed to surface? No, I suspect I don't. Nevertheless, the summary itself makes for eye-opening and thought-provoking reading. It's one in which, as you will see, Monroe is referred to as the "subject." A more bland way of describing Marilyn Monroe there probably has never been.

The document acquired by Milo Speriglio from Timothy Cooper, and which has its title excised, reads as follows:

> *Rothberg discussed the apparent comeback of subject with Kilgallen and the break up with the Kennedy's. Rothberg told Kilgallen that subject was attending Hollywood parties hosted by Hollywood's elite and was becoming the talk of the town again. Rothberg indicated in so many words, that*

TOP SECRET   NOT FOR PUBLICATI[ON]

COUNTRY ... New York, US   REPORT NO.

SUBJECT [Marilyn Monroe]   DATE DISTR 3 August 1962

NO. PAGES

REFERENCES MOON, DUST Project

3 August 1962

Wiretap of telephone [redacted] Kilgallen and b[er] close friend, Howard Rothberg (A); from wiretap of telephone conversation of Marilyn Monroe and Attorney General Robert Kennedy (B). Appraisal of Content:

1. Rothberg discussed the apparent break of subject with Kilgallen and the break up with the Kennedys. Rothberg told Kilgallen that she was attending Hollywood parties hosted by the "inner circle" among Hollywood's elite and was becoming the talk of the town again. Rothberg indicated in so many words, that she had secrets to tell, no doubt arising from her trists with the President and the Attorney General. One such "secret" mentions the visit by the President at a secret air base for the purpose of inspecting things from outer space. Kilgallen replied that she knew what might be the source of visit. In the mid-fifties Kilgallen learned of secret effort by US and UK governments to identify the origins of crashed spacecraft and dead bodies, from a British government official. Kilgallen believed the story may have come from the New York source in the late forties. Kilgall[en] said that if the story is true, it would cause terrible embarras[sment] [for] Jack and his plans to have NASA put men on the Moon.

2. Subject repeatedly called the Attorney General and complained about the w[ay] she was being ignored by the President and his brother.

3. Subject threatened to hold a press conference and would <u>tell all</u>.

4. Subject made reference to ["bases"] in Cuba and knew of the President's plan to [kill Castro.]

5. Subject made reference to her ["diary of secrets"] and what the newspapers would do with such disclosures.

TOP SECRET

According to leaked CIA documentation, President John F. Kennedy told Marilyn Monroe of his secret knowledge of "things from space." ©Unknown 1962.

subject had secrets to tell, no doubt arising from her trysts with the President and the Attorney General. One such 'secret' mentioned the visit by the President at a secret air base for the purpose of inspecting things from outer space. Kilgallen replied that she knew what might be the source of the visit. In the mid-fifties Kilgallen learned of a secret effort by US and UK governments to identify the origins of crashed spacecraft and dead bodies, from a British Government official. Kilgallen believed the story may have come from the New Mexico area in the late forties. Kilgallen said that if the story is true, it would cause terrible embarrassment for Jack and his plans to have NASA put me on the moon ("The Marilyn Monroe CIA Memo," 2013).

Subject repeatedly called the Attorney General and complained about the way she was being ignored by the President and his brother (Ibid.).

Subject threatened to hold a press conference and would tell all (Ibid.).

Subject made references to bases in Cuba and knew of the President's plan to kill Castro (Ibid.).

Subject made reference to her 'diary of secrets' and what the newspapers would do with such disclosures (Ibid.).

DISSECTING THE DOCUMENT

Given the definitive cloak and dagger fashion under which the document allegedly surfaced from a Deep Throat–type source within government to Timothy Cooper, the big question is: Can its contents be authenticated? Donald Wolfe, an investigator and writer who spent a lot of time digging into the circumstances surrounding the untimely death of Marilyn, notes that Howard Rothberg was a friend to a man named Ron Pataky, who worked for an Ohio-based newspaper, the *Columbus Citizen-Journal.*

Pataky was also a friend to Robert Slatzer, who, in 1956, was secretly told of the secret evening that Monroe spent with Indonesia's President Sukarno. In an interview with Wolfe, Pataky admitted: "Oh yes, I was very aware of [Slatzer's] longstanding relationship with Marilyn." Pataky also recalled how, in the final few weeks before Monroe's death, Slatzer received telephone calls from her, in which she discussed the "trouble" she was having with both JFK and RFK. Though the exact details were not revealed by Pataky, he did state that whatever was discussed left Slatzer "very worried." Interestingly, when Pataky was asked if he had ever spoken with Dorothy Kilgallen or Howard Rothberg about the problems Monroe was having with the Kennedy brothers, he guardedly replied: "I may have" (Wolfe, 1999).

In addition, it is a fact that Dorothy Kilgallen had, herself, a link to the UFO controversy. On May 23, 1955, the *Los Angeles Examiner* newspaper published an article from Kilgallen that revealed how, only a few days earlier, a person described as being a "British official of Cabinet rank" had informed her that the British government had gotten its hands on the remains of a crashed UFO that had been piloted by what were only, albeit tantalizingly, described as "small men." An "official report" had been secretly prepared on this extraordinary development, Kilgallen was told. She added in her article, however, that the mysterious and confidential source had advised her that the report was being withheld by British officials to avoid alarming the general public. So we have circumstances and we have people, all interconnected, and in roundabout fashion, all linked to the development and discussion of the same story related within the Speriglio document and regarding Marilyn Monroe. The affair, however, does not end there (Kilgallen, 1955).

MOON DUST SECRETS

At the top of the document, the following words appear: "Reference: MOON DUST Project." It transpires that Project Moon Dust *was* a legitimate U.S. military program, one that was highly classified in 1962. It was directed towards the careful capture and analysis of crashed Soviet space satellites and rocket debris. There are indications, too, that Moon Dust's work may have extended into far stranger—and possibly even extraterrestrial—realms. A November 1961 Air Force Intelligence document pertaining to the activities of, and guidelines for, Moon Dust personnel, specifically at their base of operations within the 1127th Air Activities Group at Fort Belvoir (known in other incarnations as the 4602nd Air Intelligence Service Squadron, and the 1006th Air Intelligence Service Squadron), carefully outlined the nature and the scope of Moon Dust, as well as that of a related program known as Blue Fly (Department of the Air Force, 1961).

Titled *AFCIN Intelligence Team Personnel*, the document revealed that, with respect to the 1127th Air Activities Group: "In addition to their staff duty assignments, intelligence team personnel have peacetime duty functions in support of such Air Force projects as Moon Dust, Blue Fly, and UFO, and other AFCIN directed quick reaction projects which require intelligence team operational capabilities" (Ibid.).

The author of the document added:

Unidentified Flying Objects (UFO): Headquarters USAF has established a program for investigation of reliably reported unidentified flying objects within the United States. Blue Fly: Operation Blue Fly has been established to facilitate expeditious delivery to Foreign Technology Division of Moon Dust or other items of great technical interest. Moon Dust: As a specialized aspect of its overall material exploitation program Headquarters USAF has established Project Moon Dust to locate, recover, and deliver descended foreign space vehicles (Ibid.).

What is particularly interesting, but seldom noted or commented upon by UFO researchers, is the fact that if the document acquired by Milo Speriglio *is* a hoax, and the primary goal was to suggest Marilyn Monroe was going to spill the beans on what the government knew about crashed flying saucers and dead aliens at Roswell, then the hoaxer behind it did not go out of his or her way to aggressively reinforce the UFO angle at all. Despite what Speriglio publicly claimed back in 1995, the document actually makes no mention whatsoever of aliens, of the controversial Roswell event, or of spaceships from faraway planets.

Yes, the Project Moon Dust reference is certainly suggestive of, at least, a potential UFO link; however, because Moon Dust's chief task was the secret acquisition of Soviet rocket- and space-based technology, a most reasonable argument can be made that the vaguely worded notes on things from outer space, crashed spacecraft, and dead bodies were references to failed, manned, Soviet rocket launches in the early years of space exploration, and *not* to aliens. Remember, too, the document also states that if the tale told to Monroe was verified, it would provoke major embarrassment for the president and his goal to have NASA land astronauts on the Moon. How the government having a crashed UFO, and a number of alien corpses on ice, might cause embarrassment to the Moon landing program makes little sense. But for America to possess secret evidence that the Soviets had launched classified manned flights into space—flights far in advance of anything that the United States might have been working on at the time—well, that could certainly have caused a lot of embarrassment.

In other words, if just an audacious hoax on the field of Ufology and nothing else, why not make specific and undeniable references to *alien* bodies instead of just *dead* bodies? And why not refer to *extraterrestrial* spacecraft instead of simply *crashed* spacecraft? Keeping those questions in mind, one can suggest that, whatever its provenance may ultimately prove to be, a fair degree of subtlety was at work in the production of the document.

The CIA does admit to having the Milo Speriglio/Timothy Cooper document on file; however, agency staff qualifies this by stating the only reason the document can be found in the archives of the CIA is because UFO researchers have mailed copies of the document to its headquarters at Langley, Virginia, inquiring about its genuineness. As for any surrounding documentation concerning this intriguing piece of paper, the CIA says that it has been unable to locate any responsive documents.

Mind you, we know for sure that the FBI definitely shared its 1950s-era files on Monroe with the CIA (they can be accessed at the Vault Website), and the latter can't find those documents either. So the CIA's stance is not exactly what one might consider firmly cast in stone. The CIA does, however, admit to having a surveillance file on Dorothy Kilgallen. Plus, that particular file covers the same time period when Kilgallen became exposed to the UFO phenomenon: 1955. Notably, although certain and select portions of the CIA dossier on Kilgallen have been declassified according to Freedom of Information regulations, other sections assuredly have not. Those redacted and denied papers are, not surprisingly, classified for what are termed national security reasons.

Now we come to one of the most notable cases of missing paper in this deeply strange saga. It all revolves around the far from insignificant matter of what the document acquired by Milo Speriglio refers to as Marilyn Monroe's diary of secrets.

A PRICELESS JOURNAL VANISHES

That the document reportedly leaked to Timothy Cooper made references to Marilyn Monroe's diary and what the press would do with such revelations, has led many a conspiracy theorist to suggest the Hollywood legend was coldly murdered before she could tell the world what she really knew on the matter of the U.S. government's most guarded secrets, perhaps even those revolving around certain, curious things from space. Maybe that is indeed exactly what happened. If not a case of suicide, theories for the culprit, or culprits, include the FBI, the CIA, the Mafia, Robert Kennedy himself, and rogue intelligence agents following personal, unofficially-authorized agendas. Whatever the case, those responsible for such a terrible act would surely not have left Monroe's personal diary lying around if, or when, they found it. And guess what? The diary is indeed missing. Nevertheless, a notable amount of data on how and why it came to vanish can be gleaned from studying the collective words of those who knew Marilyn, as well as those who were involved in the circumstances that immediately followed her death.

It was Monroe's second husband, baseball legend Joe DiMaggio, who encouraged her to keep a diary. Maybe, in a roundabout way, it was Monroe's decision to do exactly that which sealed her sad and early fate. By all accounts, the diary was a very bulky one—far more like a thick journal than something in which a person might just jot down reminders about birthdays, holidays, and so on. It was red in color and leather-bound. Dr. Jack Hattem, who has worked hard to unravel the nature of Monroe's death, says the diary contained "pillow talk," much of which involved attorney general Robert Kennedy. Hattem also notes that "the CIA long considered Marilyn Monroe a threat to national security from the time she had married Arthur Miller, because they thought of him as a leftist" (Hecklerspray staff, 2008).

Robert Slatzer says that he actually saw the diary only a couple of days before Monroe's death, and distinctly recalls that it highlighted certain conversations between the actress and Robert Kennedy. Lionel Grandison, who held the position of coroner's aid in the Los Angeles coroner's office involved in the investigation of Monroe's death, claims that he personally witnessed the diary as it was checked into the office. Only 48 hours later, however, it had mysteriously vanished. Fortunately, says Grandison, he had the opportunity to take a look at the diary. He stated, intriguingly, that it contained what was described as bizarre information. Perhaps we might consider references to dead bodies and crashed spacecraft to be fairly bizarre. And there are also the words of Mike Rothmiller, a detective with the Los Angeles Police Department and a member of its elite Organized Crime Intelligence Division. He went on the record as stating that he, too, had knowledge of the diary and said it contained references to Frank Sinatra, the Mafia, Cuba, and the former Soviet Union. Despite offers of up to a staggering $150,000 for Marilyn Monroe's secret-filled diary, it remains stubbornly missing. Or sitting in a vault somewhere, one protected by an unsmiling minion of government with a license to kill.

Clearly, in the turbulent world of Marilyn Monroe, we see deep evidence of official, secret interest in her short life, her friends, her husbands, her lovers, and even her personal diary. But we see something else, too, something central to the theme of this entire book: the large-scale disappearance of (a) classified CIA documentation on the Hollywood glamour-girl and (b) her priceless journal. Whether strategically hidden from public view, or shredded years ago to bury certain classified truths that officialdom prefer we never get to learn about, the "Monroe file" is notable not so much because of what it says, but because it's inaccessible.

And that's also true of a certain other internationally famous name and face, as we shall now see.

8: SQUIDGYGATE AND SECRET TAPES

The death of Diana, Princess of Wales, in a horrific car crash in Paris, France on August 31, 1997—along with her lover, Dodi Fayed, and driver Henri Paul—was an event that shocked the entire world. It was also an event about which many people had profound suspicions—namely, that the car accident that claimed three lives was perhaps not an accident, after all. Rather, conspiracy theorists maintain, it may have been a case of nothing less than stone-cold assassination. The reason: to ensure that Diana did not marry Fayed, an Egyptian Muslim. For the British Royal Family and the government alike, the theory goes, there was absolutely no way that the heir to the throne, Prince William (as well as his brother, Prince Harry), could be raised in part by a Muslim. Such a thing was seen as being inconceivable to the establishment. So the countdown was on to take both Diana and Fayed out of circulation. *Forever*. The result: murder by British agents (acting on official orders, or gone rogue, remains to be seen) in Paris' Pont de l'Alma tunnel on the night of the 31st.

The official verdict is that the deaths of Diana, Dodi Fayed, and Henri Paul were due to a combination of factors that resulted in disaster: (a) Paul was said to be drunk; (b) he was driving at high speed; (c) neither Diana nor Fayed were wearing seatbelts; and (d) Paul was racing through the streets at night trying to escape the pursuing paparazzi. Put all of those issues together, says officialdom, and you have a terrible, tragic accident just waiting to happen and absolutely nothing else. Nevertheless, debate continues to rage with regard to the accident vs. murder issue. One of the reasons why the matter refuses to roll over and die is because in the years leading up to the death of Diana, she was watched very closely by the security and intelligence services of several nations. She was also the subject of clandestine telephone surveillance. Not only that, Diana confided in friends that she feared she was going to die in the very fashion she ultimately did. And of specific relevance to the subject of this book, certain agencies of government and the intelligence services have admitted to having files on Princess Diana that they refuse to release into the public domain. No wonder that many look at the nature of Princess Diana's death through suspicious and cynical eyes.

SECRET AFFAIRS, SECRET SURVEILLANCE, SECRET FILES

There is strong evidence available suggesting that when Diana's marriage to Prince Charles was not going well—from the mid-1980s onward—she began to look around for someone to have a bit of fun with on the side. Several people on several sides, actually. One of those, the rumor mill suggests, was a man named Barry Mannakee. The British Police Force has a directorate called Special Operations, under which there is a division called the Protection Command. Within that, there is yet another body. Its title is the Royalty Protection Branch, otherwise known as SO14. As its name implies, this is the group that coordinates all police-based operations designed to protect the Royal Family. Barry Mannakee was a member of this important and elite group, and was assigned as Diana's bodyguard in 1985. The pair quickly became friends. They may ultimately have become far more than that. It's known that Diana often confided in Mannakee about the state of her private life, her less-than-happy marriage to Prince Charles, and her many and varied personal woes. But, according to some, that shoulder to cry on soon developed into something else. A longstanding story tells of one Colin Trimming—who was Prince Charles's personal protection officer at the time—walking in on Mannakee and seeing something he preferred not to have. The result was that, in 1986, Mannakee was transferred to other duties. That didn't stop Diana from chatting with, and also meeting, Mannakee. But something did. It was something that ensured the two never had any contact ever again.

On the evening of May 14, 1987, Barry Mannakee was killed in a traffic accident in the south Woodford district of Essex. He was the passenger on a motorbike driven by a friend and colleague, Steven Peat, which collided with a car that turned into the bike's path. There was no time or room for anything

Was the death of Princess Diana (second from left) in 1997 an accident or murder? ©U.S. Government, 1985

but a deadly collision. Mannakee's spine was broken in two places after he was thrown from the bike and straight through the rear driver's-side window of the car. The young woman behind the wheel of the car, Nicola Chopp, received a small fine for driving without due care and attention. Interestingly, at the inquest, testimony was revealed suggesting the presence of an unknown car and driver at the scene. Reportedly, the car in question possessed extremely dazzling lights that may have temporarily blinded those involved in the accident. Notably, there is a story that Princess Diana's death in the Pont de l'Alma tunnel was prompted by the use of a high-powered strobe-light weapon, one that emitted a blinding flash and led Henri Paul to slam into the tunnel's 13th pillar at 65 mph. Supposedly, the device was something developed by MI6 to dazzle and disorient enemy helicopter pilots during warfare. And on the matter of MI6, allegations exist that Henri Paul was in their unofficial employ. Then there's the issue of an alleged missing file on the Mannakee affair.

Charles Ronald George Nall-Cain is better known as the 3rd Baron Brocket. In March 1998, while serving two and a half years in Britain's Springhill Open Prison for insurance fraud, he claimed to have been told by a fellow prisoner—a former police officer also inside for fraud—that there existed a classified file on Mannakee's death. It was a file that allegedly concluded that the motorbike had been tampered with prior to the accident. The revelations came about, Brocket maintained, when he and the officer got into conversation about Diana's death. Of course, that the story came from a convicted fraudster, who claimed to have gotten it from an unknown former police officer (who also happened to be a convicted fraudster), makes it difficult to prove anything. But, regardless of the truth of the secret file, even Diana herself admitted to suspecting that Manna-kee's death was not the accident it seemed to be. And the stories of secret files in relation to Princess Diana do not end there.

In the summer of 1986, Princess Diana began a clandestine, on-and-off affair with one Major James Hewitt that lasted for around five years in total. Formerly a British Household Cavalry Officer with the British Army, Hewitt served as a tank commander in the first Gulf War. During the course of their affair, both Diana and Hewitt were put under close physical surveillance by the Intelligence Corps of the British Army. The reason being to ensure that Diana—while secretly visiting the home of Hewitt, in the Devonshire, England, village of Bratton Clovelly—was not kidnapped or killed by the Irish Republican Army (IRA) who, it was feared, had somehow uncovered scant details of the affair from sources still unknown.

Jonathan Downes is an English author who went to school with Hewitt and who, as a result, knows Bratton Clovelly very well. In addition, Downes's father and brother were both decorated by Queen Elizabeth II. In the late 1980s—long before the details of the Hewitt-Diana affair became public knowledge—Downes learned from a military intelligence contact that the pair was being watched and that extensive dossiers existed on their secret liaisons in Bratton Clovelly. Hardly jaw-dropping is the fact that those Army Intelligence dossiers have not surfaced into the public domain.

THE TWIST-FILLED TALE OF THE SQUIDGYGATE TAPES

Another of those who Diana is rumored to have had an affair with is a man named James Gilbey, a PR executive and a great-nephew of Monsignor Alfred Gilbey, a Roman Catholic theologian. Although Gilbey has never confirmed nor denied anything more than a friendship with Diana that echoed back to their younger days, his name has forever been linked with her for one famous reason. Actually, it's more infamous than it is famous. It's noted for its deep conspiracy links, too. It has become known as Squidgygate, a play on words of the equally infamous Watergate scandal that rocked the United States in the 1970s and that will be addressed in a later chapter. And what a strange and convoluted affair Squidgygate was.

Things all began on January 4, 1990, with a man named Cyril Reenan. Hailing from the ancient English town of Abingdon, Oxfordshire, Reenan was a retired bank manager. He and his wife had an interesting, albeit slightly alternative, way of passing the hours. The Reenans put together a collection of equipment that allowed them to scan the airwaves and eavesdrop on just about anyone whose conversations could be detected. This included tapping into police frequencies, two-way radios, and some of the large, brick-like cell phones that existed back then. It was while Reenan was entertaining himself by listening in to, and even recording, private chatter that he got the shock of his life. To Reenan's amazement and concern, it was a conversation between Princess Diana and James Gilbey.

Throughout the recording, Gilbey playfully referred to Diana as Squidge and Squidgy. The subject matters of the conversation were highly entertaining and illuminating. Diana expressed her loathing for the Royal Family, said that the Queen Mother viewed her with a mixture of pity and interest, and confided in Gilbey that she thought she might be pregnant; by who, however, was not made clear. A moaning Diana said that Prince Charles made her life torturous, and she likened her turbulent existence to that of some of the characters from the long-running BBC soap opera, *Eastenders*.

Reenan was both excited and more than a bit concerned by what had fallen into his lap as a result of nosing his way around the nation's airwaves. It didn't take Reenan long to come to a decision about what he should do. After initially thinking about, and then rejecting, the idea of trying to contact the princess himself (to help her save face, so he said), Reenan decided to phone the offices of Britain's most famous tabloid newspaper, the *Sun*. Precisely how putting a tabloid newspaper onto the story might have helped Diana's position is anyone's guess. Within days, a couple of eager journalists from the newspaper met with Reenan to try to get to the bottom of things. A by-now deeply worried Reenan, who was having second thoughts about bringing the media into the situation, was glad to be rid of the tape and quickly handed it over to the eager and enthusiastic reporters. In return, he received 6000 English pounds.

It was not until August 24, 1992, that the *Sun* ran the story of the tape, the conversation between Diana and Gilbey, and Reenan's role in the matter—the newspaper's staff having quietly and carefully investigated the whole matter for more than one and a half years. The timing was interesting. Apparently, from sources still unknown, the American *National Enquirer* tabloid had just received *another* copy of the tape. When the *Sun's* staff got word of this, and understandably became fearful of losing its big scoop, it was full steam ahead to get the story out immediately. It caused a nationwide sensation and rocked

Buckingham Palace to its foundations. But the reporters assigned to the story uncovered something most weird along the way. The conversation that Reenan claimed he recorded on January 4, 1990, actually took place on December 31, 1989: New Year's Eve. That much was in evidence from the specific words that can be heard in the recording.

Not only that, yet another Oxfordshire resident, Jane Norgrove, also recorded the same conversation, but four days *before* Reenan, thereby further bolstering the December 31st date as being the correct one. According to Norgrove, she didn't even listen to the tape at the time it was recorded. It was, she said, only weeks later when she finally played it and, to her amazement, realized to whose voice she was listening. Roughly a year on—January 1991—Norgrove, very oddly, just like Reenan, approached the *Sun* with her version of the Diana-Gilbey exchange. But how could one conversation, between two people, presumably going out live, get picked up *twice* across a period of four days? Here's where things get murky.

TAMPERING WITH A TAPE

First and foremost, it should be noted that cell phones, in 1989, were hardly the things they are today, in terms of ability and reception. Yet, the recording between Diana and Gilbey—which occurred when the two were more than 100 miles apart—was crystal clear. William Parsons, of Systems Elite, a company that consulted for clients that wanted to make sure they were not the victims of surveillance, said that he did not believe it was possible that Reenan had picked up the conversation by accident. There just had to have been far more afoot, Parsons added. His words turned out to be prophetic and bang on target.

One year after the *Sun* broke the story, a firm called Audiotel International analyzed the recording and noted something significant: On the tape, certain so-called data bursts could be heard, at intervals of 10 seconds. Such bursts contained data used in the billing process by the company that made Gilbey's cell phone, which was called Cellnet. Those same bursts, however, would not normally be audible on the conversation, only to the staff of Cellnet. On top of that, the recording, said Andrew Martin, the managing director of Audiotel, also contained a low frequency shadow, which suggested the tape had been doctored to some uncertain degree. Martin's conclusion was that the conversation between Diana and Gilbey had been recorded at its source—which was either Gilbey's cell phone or Diana's private number at Sandringham House, Norfolk. Then, suggested Martin, it was broadcast in an altered fashion, and using a technology that allowed it to be picked up by the scanning equipment of Reenan and Norgrove. The big questions were: Whose phone was being tapped,

Diana's or Gilbey's? Might it even have been both? And why, precisely, was some-one going to the trouble of broadcasting the conversation in the first place?

Most experts that examined and studied the recording concluded it was Diana's phone that was being monitored and the bug was at her end—either within the actual phone itself or at the nearest exchange. Another revelation surfaced. At the time both Norgrove and Reenan picked up the conversation, Gilbey was using a phone purchased from Cellnet. Why is this important? Simple: Cellnet did not have a transmitter in the Abingdon area until March 1990—two months after Reenan recorded the chat. In other words, even if it was Gilbey's phone that was tapped, there was no way that Reenan could have picked up the call in a town where there was no Cellnet transmitter.

On top of that, Cellnet, obviously wanting to protect its own image, con-ducted an inquiry and determined that the recording was not the result of its system being compromised, but a case of one of the two chatting parties being bugged. And where was the nearest telephone exchange to Sandringham? It was actually *inside* the house itself. Someone was clandestinely listening in on Diana, and potentially all the time. As for why the guilty party chose to broadcast the recording in the vicinity of the home of Reenan, well, that may be because he had a 20-foot-high aerial in his garden and was known locally as someone who liked to listen in on private conversations.

That is, someone dearly wanted the details of the conversation between Diana and Gilbey to become public knowledge. And they wanted to do it in a fashion that didn't compromise their identity, but in a way that made it seem as if Reenan had picked up the conversation all on his own and by pure chance. That checks of Reenan's somewhat antiquated equipment demonstrated there was no way he could have intercepted a call made on a Cellnet line, in an area where no Cellnet transmitter existed, reveals the biggest error on the part of whoever perpetrated this brilliant, yet ultimately flawed, operation. As for the reason, it was clearly done to have an adverse effect upon Diana's character, particularly so when the media got hold of it, all thanks to Reenan running to the *Sun*, eagerly taking their six grand in exchange for the tape, and running back to the safety and privacy of his home. It's a big shame that Reenan didn't think more about affording Diana that same privacy.

POINTING THE FINGER AT THE GUILTY PARTIES

There does not appear to be any evidence suggesting Reenan and Norgrove were anything but innocent players in this almost surreal affair, albeit ones who decided to go to the newspapers with what they had stumbled upon. Although, it is interesting that a cagey Reenan once admitted there was a great deal more about the story of the tape that had never surfaced. It was a statement he steadfastly declined to elaborate on. Not only that, Reenan did a lot of work for charity, and, as a result, was the recipient of an award from none other than the Princess of Wales' Charity Trust. Given that Reenan had a link to Diana, in a roundabout way, that he knew her voice, and that he possessed eavesdropping and recording equipment, may have made him the ideal patsy to try to get the recording into the public domain. This suggests, too, that a great deal of behind-the-scenes planning must have gone on to find someone like Reenan, who fit the bill to the proverbial tee.

As for who, exactly, the guilty party may have been, most fingers were pointed in the direction of the Government Communications Headquarters (GCHQ), which is based in the English town of Cheltenham. Calls made by cell phones and landlines, e-mails, faxes, and just about every other form of electronic communication under the sun are routinely intercepted and analyzed by GCHQ's staff, all in the name of what passes for national security. Ken Wharfe, Diana's bodyguard from 1987 to 1993, outright accused GCHQ of being the culprits. The reason, Wharfe suggested, was heightened activity at the time on the part of the Irish Republican Army. This, of course, echoes closely the story told to Jonathan Downes in the late 1980s concerning Diana's affair with James Hewitt, and fears of IRA attempts to either kidnap or kill the princess. Perhaps predictably, staff at GCHQ denied such accusations, as did both MI5 and MI6. This, however, didn't stop Queen Elizabeth from demanding that MI5 launch an inquiry.

Today, the Squidgygate affair remains the enigma that it was two decades ago. Jane Norgrove is saying nothing. Cyril Reenan went to his grave, at the age of 82 in 2004, never having revealed anything more than he did a decade or so earlier for a fistful of English pounds. But the fact remains that someone, somewhere, possessed the skills and technology to bug Princess Diana's telephone. That the phone was inside Sandringham House, one of the UK's most well-guarded places, makes it all the more likely that this was a professional operation run by the cream of Britain's security services. That same someone then skillfully doctored a conversation between Diana and James Gilbey, and then broadcast it—twice, no less—near the home of an old man who was all but guaranteed to hear it, and possibly even do something with it. As he did— namely, to hand it over to Britain's leading tabloid newspaper, whose staff gleefully dished the dirt all across the land.

As for MI5's investigation, it's yet another case of for nobody's eyes only. The results of the inquiry remain locked behind closed doors. But we may, at least, be able to glean some insight into the contents of the report from the words of Ken Wharfe. He claimed that MI5's investigation did identify all the players in the affair but, as a result of certain legal factors, he was unable to elaborate further. Wharfe was willing to add, however, that the results of the investigation strongly supported Princess Diana's suspicions that powerful figures wanted her gone.

And what about those tapes of Diana's conversations with James Gilbey? What happened to the original recording? Nobody knows. That is, except for those technical wizards that recorded it, then meddled with it, and finally rebroadcast it across the English town of Abingdon as 1989 turned into 1990. Perhaps it was tossed into a blazing furnace. Maybe it was pulverized into tiny pieces. Or, perhaps, it is deep underground, stored far away from those who are deemed unfit and unworthy to access it. (That's the rest of us, by the way.) We can never really be sure. What we can be certain of is the fact that it was not just British Intelligence that had Princess Diana in its sights. So did America's secret agents.

U.S. SPIES WATCH DIANA

In the final weeks of 1998, the U.S. National Security Agency confirmed that it possessed more than 1,000 pages of classified documents on Princess Diana. That numerous people perceived Diana's death as being something more than a tragic accident, prompted a lot of debate about what, precisely, those NSA files contained. The NSA chose not to provide much by way of an answer. Still, that didn't stop Britain's popular, mainstream newspapers from having their say. The *Daily Mirror* suggested the material was being withheld because its release would confirm Diana's secret affairs during her marriage to Prince Charles. The *Daily Record* theorized that the files, if declassified, might show the full and shocking extent to which the NSA had spied on Diana—possibly right up until her death in 1997. The *Washington Post* took a less sensational view. It opined that the truth of the NSA's surveillance was likely far less lurid than suggested by the British press. The *Post* added some useful data, which outlined at least some of the facts relative to what was being withheld from public view. As the newspaper noted, although the NSA refused to release its files on Diana, it did confirm that one such file amounted to 1,056 pages, and that 39 additional files totaling 124 pages also existed. Those particular records, the NSA was at least willing to admit, were deemed non-releasable for national security reasons relative to how the agency undertakes its surveillance operations.

For years, the CIA compiled secret files on Princess Diana. They remain classified. ©CIA

The National Security Agency is not the only U.S. government agency that has admitted to possessing files related to Princess Diana that it flatly refuses to declassify. The CIA has an undisclosed number of records on file, which might, therefore, mean 10 or 10,000; we just don't know. The Defense Intelligence Agency (DIA) confirms it has what it hazily describes as information and product on Diana. When pressed for answers concerning the matter of why, exactly, the DIA might have classified product (whatever that might mean) on Diana, a DIA spokesperson, Lt. Col. James McNeil, did not shy away from saying he had not a clue. He did add that the work of the DIA was focused on military matters, and he noted that Diana was certainly not in the employ of the military. No, Diana *wasn't* in the military. She *was*, however, an active campaigner in the effort to have landlines made illegal. The world's defense contractors, who made fortunes out of landmine sales, were far from happy that someone as vocal and visible as Diana wanted to see their products banned. Of course, when she died, so did her vigorous campaigning.

Notably, in 1999, Britain's *Guardian* newspaper, which had been digging into the matter of the NSA's papers on Diana, uncovered something very interesting: A number of the files that the National Security Agency possessed on Diana had been forwarded to the American eavesdropping agency by MI5 and MI6. Not only that, they were also classified Top Secret. The *Guardian* noted that, of the discoveries its reporters had made, the files were not focused so much on Diana herself, but on certain company that she kept. Perhaps, from that, we can deduce this was a reference to Barry Mannakee, James Gilbey, and James Hewitt.

Might we imply from all of the above that the NSA knows at least some of the truth of the Squidgygate affair? Maybe the answer is yes. In fairly bureaucratic terms, the NSA has admitted that although it does not monitor the activities of British citizens, it was not out of the question that the intelligence services of the UK might share data with the NSA that British agents had specifically acquired. That's a very roundabout way of saying the NSA could well have *masses* of material on Diana and other British individuals, even if its staff didn't personally compile that same material.

Someone, surely, knows the full truth of Squidgygate. Maybe those people are hidden deep in the world of British intelligence. Perhaps a few trusted colleagues across the pond know the complete story, too. But, when MI5, the CIA, the NSA, and the DIA flatly, and collectively, refuse to reveal what they have on file regarding Princess Diana, her private life, and her tragic death, we know for sure who *isn't* in on the full story: us.

And there's one more person to focus on whose files no one on the inside wants us to see. It was a man who was downright infamously devilish.

9: A CELEBRITY SORCERER GOES SPYING

Born in 1875, in Leamington, England, Aleister Crowley was, and for many still is, the ultimate occultist. He's also a man who, decades after his death in 1947, has developed a significant and devoted following in the world of the rich and famous. Led Zeppelin guitarist Jimmy Page once lived in an old and creepy house that Crowley owned. Its name is Boleskine House, and it is located on the shores of Scotland's infamous and equally creepy Loch Ness. Former Black Sabbath vocalist and reality TV star, Ozzy Osbourne, co-wrote a song about the master magician titled "Mr. Crowley." The magician's photo appears on the cover of the Beatles' 1967 album, *Sgt. Pepper's Lonely Hearts Club Band*. And a bust of the man himself can be seen on the back cover of the Doors' 1970 compilation record, *13*. Add to that various references to Crowley in the musical output of David Bowie, and you have a man and an occultist with near-rock-star-like status and legend. But there's far more than that to the man who Ozzy made famous.

Aleister Crowley, also famously referred to as the Great Beast, was someone who harbored a profound and amazing secret: For years he worked in an undercover, and unofficial, capacity for British intelligence. Don't, however, expect the British government to confirm this or release any secret files anytime soon on its relationship with, and to, Crowley. Never mind. British officials may have deemed us unworthy of knowing the magic-filled truth, but that doesn't mean we can't uncover that same truth via good old investigative

Aleister Crowley, an infamous occult-ist and a secret agent of the British government. ©Unknown 1912

techniques. Before we get to this latter point, though, let's head back to the beginnings of the Beast.

FROM THE CHURCH TO THE LOCH

Aleister Crowley was the son of a noted brewer and, ironically, someone who was brought up in a devout Christian environment and taught in an evangelist school. This was hardly surprising, given that his father, Edward, was a full-brown preacher. We can, perhaps, deduce from all of this that young Aleister, when he began to look in distinctly different areas for spiritual comfort and enlightenment, was demonstrating far more than a youthful, spirited rebellion. Certainly, by his teens Crowley was already displaying a deep interest in, and a fascination for, magical rituals and the ancient secrets of alchemy. At the age of 22, he joined a body called the Hermetic Order of the Golden Dawn, a magical order that was founded in Great Britain during the late 19th century. It practiced theurgy, which, essentially, is the process of using complex rites and rituals to command an audience with a supernatural entity or deity. One of those who taught Crowley a great deal about theurgy was a man named Alan Bennett. He was a member of the Golden Dawn, and someone from whom Crowley learned much about strange and dark realms beyond our own, and how the uncanny things that inhabited these other realms could be summoned forth. Crowley also developed an enthusiastic passion for travel, which took him to such diverse locations as Paris, London, and Mexico, the latter where he achieved the status of a 33rd Degree Mason.

As the 20th century began, and as he reached the age of 25, Crowley headed off to the wilds of Scotland and the home of the world's most famous lake-monster: Loch Ness. While at Boleskine House—which backed onto an equally old and atmosphere-filled cemetery, a place where it was rumored an ancient witch coven practiced its dark and evil rites—Crowley wasted no time in living life to the full. Weekend-long, wild sex parties and midnight rites held on the shores of the ancient loch were just two of the many highlights. Some of the paranormal phenomena that Crowley allegedly conjured up at Boleskine House supposedly led a maid to flee in terror, never to return. A local workman who did chores for Crowley reportedly went completely mad. Then there was the butcher from a nearby village who died while slicing meat. He carelessly severed an artery and bled to death on the cold, stone floor of his own shop. This was no accident, claimed Crowley. How did he know this? Simple, according to the man himself: The butcher had billed him for a quantity of meat; but instead of paying the bill—as most of us would do—Crowley chose to write the names of various demonic entities on the bill and send far more than a bit of negative and lethal energy in the direction of the butcher's workplace.

A SCARLET WOMAN AND A THING CALLED LAM

For the first three months of 1918, Crowley was on the receiving end of various messages that, in essence, were telepathically transferred to him by a woman named Roddie Minor, or as Crowley preferred to call her, his scarlet woman. History has shown she was not Crowley's only scarlet woman, but she was certainly one of the most significant—and for a very good reason: Minor's messages were reportedly coming from supernatural entities that varied wildly from the demonic to the angelic. Crowley wasn't interested in just receiving messages, however. Echoing back to his theurgy-based studies of the late 1800s, Crowley was wholly intent on using ritual and rite to actually call forth the entities behind the messages and, then, have those same entities manifest before him. Crowley knew more than enough of the occult world to say for sure that the old adage of "be careful what you ask for" held true, ominously so, too. Unlocking and then opening the doors to dimensions very different to ours was one thing. But successfully banishing back to those same dimensions whatever kind of paranormal creature might come through was another matter entirely. Nevertheless, Crowley was not one to be deterred so easily. As a result, he embarked on something called the Amalantrah Working.

It might sound like the plot of one of H.P. Lovecraft's most nightmarish, ghoulish tales of dark terror. According to Crowley, however, it was all too amazingly true. The Amalantrah Working saw Crowley commence upon a complicated, ancient ritual while under the influence of both mescaline and hashish—at the same time. Not surprisingly, Crowley was quickly rendered into a manifestly out of this world–style condition of consciousness. It was while in this highly altered, stoned, and trippy state that Crowley encountered

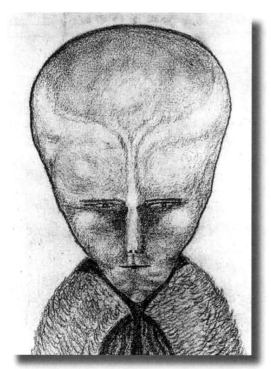

Aleister Crowley's own drawing of Lam, an invoked supernatural entity. ©Aleister Crowley

a somewhat sinister, foreboding, and judgmental-looking creature that called itself Lam. With a large bald head, penetrating eyes, and withered body, Lam was practically the identical twin of the strange, hairless entity that stares famously forth from the cover of Whitley Strieber's 1987 alien abduction-themed book, *Communion*. Crowley, however, didn't consider Lam to be an extraterrestrial in the way we understand the word today. For the magician who knew no boundaries, Lam was an Enochian entity. It was a term inspired by the Enochian Call, a language that had been developed by Dr. John Dee, a magician of renown in Britain of the 1600s. Notably, and eerily echoing the *Communion* parallels, Dee and a colleague, Edward Kelly, had their own ritual-born encounters with ominous, diminutive humanoids that soared the skies and surfed the dimensions. They did so in what Dee described as a small blazing cloud. Or in what, today, we might well term a UFO. Crowley, having invited Lam into his presence and having survived to tell the tale, was far from done with courting controversy.

CROWLEY'S DEATH: FAKERY AND REALITY

In 1930—demonstrating a flair for both controversy and black humor—Crowley decided to fake his own demise. In September of that year, he spent time in the Portuguese city of Cascais. At the appropriately named Boca do Inferno (the Mouth of Hell), a water-filled rift that sits within the seaside cliffs of the city, Crowley put his plan into action. He had help from Fernando Pessoa, an acclaimed Portuguese poet and publisher. The story was that Crowley died in the choppy waters of Boca do Inferno. It was a story that the world's media quickly reported upon. It was, however, all an outrageous lie. A highly satisfied and amused Crowley quietly and stealthily left Portugal, and duly laid low for a while. His resurrection took place three weeks later in Berlin, Germany. The dead magician, his followers were delighted to learn, was not quite as dead after all.

In 1944, as war raged across Europe and the Pacific, Crowley published a title for which he has become renowned: *The Book of Thoth*, which described his usage of, beliefs surrounding, and philosophies concerning tarot cards. It was to be his last major achievement. Crowley died on December 1, 1947, at age 72. Had it not been for serious addictions to both morphine and heroin, he might have lived longer. Regardless, Crowley's name, influence, and role in the development of 20th-century magic all live on, perhaps even within the secret-filled corridors of power, too.

CROWLEY THE SPY: THE EARLY YEARS

Created in 1883, the Primrose League was a body designed to uphold and disseminate right-wing, conservative views among the British population and the media. In other words, it acted as a kind of unofficial publicity machine. Playing a key role in the creation of the league was Lord Randolph Churchill, father to the acclaimed British prime minister Sir Winston Churchill, who successfully steered the British people through the turbulent years of the Second World War. Interestingly, the initial meeting that led to the creation of the group was held at the Carlton Club, on London's St. James's Street. A prestigious locale that was practically a second home to the movers and shakers of conservatism, the Carlton Club is, today, well known (unofficially, at least) for the many and varied employees of MI5 and MI6 that are among its elite members. That alone makes it all the more intriguing that there is a connection between Aleister Crowley and the Carlton Club. In his youth, the controversial magician was a full-blown member. Crowley's role was to spy on those powerful figures in politics that were firmly against conservative principles. Perhaps this was where Crowley got a taste for the secret world of espionage that was soon to follow.

Bolstering this possibility is a story suggesting that Crowley's decision to join the Hermetic Order of the Golden Dawn, although not undertaken at the orders of British Intelligence agents, was hardly frowned upon by leading establishment figures—and for one good purpose: Within the Golden Dawn was a man named Samuel Liddell MacGregor Mathers. He was an unusual and enigmatic character—a vegan, a Freemason, and someone vehemently against smoking (when it was practically de rigueur to puff away like a chimney).

Despite his standing with the Freemasons, who were, and still are, dominated by powerful establishment figures, Mathers is known to have harbored a secret interest in radical politics and extremism. Crowley, the story goes, was encouraged by late-19th-century English spymasters to apply at least some of his time with the Hermetic Order of the Golden Dawn to closely watching Mathers, and monitoring with whom he spoke and where he went. Ominously, Mathers died in 1918, under mysterious circumstances. Additionally, his death certificate lacked a cause of death, his body quickly vanished, and no grave or memorial stone exists for him anywhere. It was almost as if someone, perhaps someone wielding great power from within the heart of London's secret, inner world, wanted the man gone for good. And maybe they got exactly what they wanted.

Aleister Crowley didn't shy away from his bisexuality. One of those with whom he had a sexual relationship was Victor Neuberg, a publisher, poet, and writer. In 1909, Crowley and Neuberg made their first of a number of trips to Algiers, the capital of Algeria. The reason was to engage in sex-based magical rituals that followed the teachings of the aforementioned Dr. John Dee. Or was that the reason? Or maybe, more correctly, was it the *only* reason? Could it have been the case that this is what Crowley, and possibly British spies, wanted people to think? Algeria was under French rule at the time that Neuberg and Crowley were in residence. As a result, the local police, titled the Services des Affaires Indigenes, had both men solidly in their sights. They held suspicions that Crowley, in particular, was doing more than a bit of spying on the French military for the British government and using his occult-based actions as an ingenious cover story. Maybe those same police officers knew something on which, today, we can only speculate and theorize.

Around this same time, Crowley got mixed up with a man named Karl Theodor Reuss. Not only was Reuss heavily into the occult, he was also a member of the Illuminati and a Freemason. And, in the late 1800s, he just happened to work for the secret police of Prussia. This was a body so feared that it led Adolf Hitler to model the equally feared Gestapo on its ruthless methods of interrogation and data collection. One operation in which Reuss is known to have played a role occurred in London around 1885 or 1886. It was Reuss's task, at the secret orders of the Prussians, to find a way into the Socialist League to determine its funding, membership, and plans. As it was Reuss who made Crowley a member of a religion-based body, the Ordo Templi Orientis, it seems safe to say they shared a fair degree of common ground.

When the First World War broke out in 1914, Crowley played a prominent role in helping the war effort. At the time, Crowley was living—albeit just for a few years—in the United States. While in the States, Crowley made a number of vehemently anti-British statements. These were actually brilliant, collective subterfuge. The plan, drawn up by intelligence agents, was for Crowley to cultivate his seemingly traitorous character and infiltrate groups that were anti-British and pro-German, and then report back to London on what he had uncovered. To bolster the idea that Crowley was an outrageous traitor, government personnel—working with contacts in the media—inserted faked stories into the pages of influential and widely read British newspapers about his supposed lack of allegiance to Britain and the flag. The result: This significantly helped Crowley gain the trust of those pro-German figures in the United States that Crowley was actually working against. Then there was his relationship to the world of spying during the Second World War.

THE HITLER YEARS

When, in the 1930s, it became increasingly apparent to the British government that Adolf Hitler was almost certainly going to plunge Britain into a disastrous world war, Crowley was ready and willing to help. During the build up to the Second World War—which began in September 1939, after Hitler's hordes invaded Poland—Crowley became far more than a casual acquaintance to three noted individuals. Their names were Ian Fleming, Maxwell Knight, and Dennis Wheatley. In May 1939, Fleming became the personal assistant to Rear Admiral John Godfrey, the director of Britain's Naval Intelligence. As a result, Fleming moved effortlessly in the worlds of the government's clandestine Joint Intelligence Committee and the Secret Intelligence Services. Fleming's biggest, and certainly most justified, claim to fame is that he created the ultimate fictional spy, James Bond, 007.

Dennis Wheatley was a noted and acclaimed author of supernatural fiction novels, probably the most well-known of his titles being *The Devil Rides Out*. While Britain was trying to fend off Nazi hordes, however, Wheatley was playing a decisive role in the innocent-sounding London Controlling Section (LCS). One might be forgiven for thinking with a name like that it was some kind of tedious, bureaucratic arm of government. It was, however, far from that. In reality, the LCS was the primary outfit involved in coordinating deception-based operations against the Germans.

As for Maxwell Knight, he was a powerful figure within Britain's MI5. He was also partly the inspiration behind the character "M" in the James Bond novels, as penned by the aforementioned Ian Fleming. That Aleister Crowley could count on all three as not being unknown to him, speaks volumes about the man and his ability to mix easily with prominent and powerful people in the shadow-filled world of spying.

When, in 1941, the combined efforts of the Secret Intelligence Service and Naval Intelligence successfully lured Rudolf Hess—one of Hitler's leading cronies—to Britain, Ian Fleming suggested it would be a very good idea to have Crowley interview him. The reason being, Hess, like many leading Nazis, was obsessed with the world of the occult, as, of course, was Crowley. In other words, there was common ground between the two, which might have been beneficial in trying to make Hess feel comfortable when it came to the matter of extracting information from him. MI5, at least, appears not to have had a problem with this idea. Crowley reportedly did interview Hess, on two occasions, at a location somewhere in the heart of south London.

FINDING THE CROWLEY FILES IS NO EASY TASK

Richard B. Spence, a consultant to the Washington, D.C.–based International Spy Museum, and a professor of history at the University of Idaho is the one person, more than any other, who has tried to get to the heart of the connections between British intelligence and Aleister Crowley. Before we get to the matter of missing documents, it is worth noting Spence's thoughts on Crowley: "He was such a disreputable and even evil character in the public mind that arguably no responsible intelligence official would think of employing him. But the very fact that he seemed such an improbable spy was perhaps the best recommendation for using him." To be sure, those are wise words (Spence, 2008).

Spence devoted a great deal of his time trying to uncover official files on Crowley from British intelligence. It would be more than fair to say that Spence was given the definitive runaround. In early 2003, as a result of his inquiries with MI5, Spence was assured that the clandestine agency had never compiled any files on Crowley, whatsoever. That might have been just about okay, had it not been for the fact that shortly afterward a document surfaced from within Britain's National Archives—specifically a 1930s-era document generated by MI5—that referenced a file on Crowley. This was a major breakthrough—except for one thing: MI5 informed Spence, when he made inquiries about the status and nature of the referenced file, that—wait for it, you know what's coming—it could not be found. MI5's response regarding the frustratingly missing dossier was of the type that, as we have seen time and again, government staff routinely trot out when troublesome questions are asked of them. The file was supposedly destroyed in the 1950s, by which time it was perceived as being of no meaningful use or value anymore. A similar comment was made with regard to yet other file references to Crowley that Spence uncovered soon afterward.

Such a situation is mirrored in the United States. Nevertheless, regarding Crowley's time spent in the States when the First World War was raging, Spence discovered a document that originated with U.S. Army Intelligence and that may add a high degree of credence to the claims concerning his alleged espionage-based activities for the British during this period. In part, the Army's report stated clearly that Aleister Crowley was an employee of the British Government and that he was in the United States on official business, the nature of which the British Consul in New York had full awareness.

It's also worth noting that Jack Parsons—a rocket scientist and a Crowley devotee who held a Top Secret clearance with the U.S. military in the 1940s, and whose declassified file has been withdrawn from the FBI's Website—was investigated by the FBI and U.S. military intelligence in 1950. The combined files on Parsons make it clear that American officials knew all about the history that existed between Crowley and Parsons. This included the fact that, in 1942, Crowley personally chose Parsons to lead the Agape Lodge of the Ordo Templi Orientis in California. Because the FBI is the American equivalent of Britain's MI5, and MI5 is known to have put together files on Crowley (even if, MI5's staff claim, such files cannot be located today), the possibility that there may have been a transatlantic sharing of data between intelligence agencies cannot be ruled out.

But why should such seemingly extreme measures have been taken to try to expunge any evidence of Aleister Crowley's connections to the domain of international espionage at all? The Second World War was a long time ago. The First World War was even further back into 20th century history. What's the problem with sharing such old secrets in this day and age? The correct answer may well be the one that has been provided by a former U.S. intelligence officer, W. Adam Mandelbaum. He has noted that from the post–First World War era, and right up until the early part of the Second World War, Crowley "did in some capacity or other serve the needs of British Intelligence, working for MI5." Of relevance to the theme of this book—hidden and missing files— Mandelbaum says: "Given the political fallout that would have resulted from making this involvement public, it should be no surprise that there is a paucity of documentation concerning Crowley's intelligence efforts" (Mandelbaum, 2002). By now, no, it certainly is *not* a surprise!

From famous people, we now turn our attention to a collection of secret projects, the existence of which many official insiders have done their best to bury.

PART 4:
SECRET
GOVERNMENT PROJECTS

10: MISSING MORE OFTEN THAN NOT

Since the mid-1940s, various arms of the U.S. intelligence community have taken a deep interest in paranormal phenomena, including extra-sensory perception (ESP), clairvoyance, life beyond death, and precognition. For example, in 1977, Kenneth A. Kress, then attached to the CIA's Office of Technical Services, penned a paper for the agency titled "Parapsychology in Intelligence." In part, it stated: "Anecdotal reports of extrasensory perception (ESP) capabilities have reached U.S. national security agencies at least since World War II, when Hitler was said to rely on astrologers and seers. Suggestions for military applications of ESP continued to be received after World War II. For example, in 1952 the Department of Defense was lectured on the possible usefulness of extrasensory perception in psychological warfare" (Kress, 1977).

One year later, in 1953, says Dr. Nelson Pacheco, who retired from the U.S. Air Force in 1987 as a lieutenant colonel: "The CIA began infiltrating séances and occult gatherings during the 50s.... A memo dated April 9, 1953, refers to a domestic—and therefore illegal—operation that required the planting of a very specialized observer at a séance in order to obtain a broad surveillance of all individuals attending the meetings" (Pacheco and Blann, 1993).

Then there's Andrija Puharich, an American-Yugoslavian. From 1947, in his laboratory at Glen Cove, Maine, Puharich plunged himself in the study of psychic phenomena and, as a direct result, attracted some interesting people from the world of the military. In 1953, the U.S. Army's chief of the research section of the Office of the Chief of Psychological Warfare "dropped in to say hello," as Puharich somewhat amusingly worded it. Puharich also noted that his military visitor "was quite interested in a device which we had been developing in order to increase the power of extrasensory perception. The colonel then surprised me by saying that if we found any positive results to be sure to let him know, as the Army was definitely not disinterested in this kind of work." And the research continued at a steady, secret pace (Puharich, 1974).

In the late 1950s, J. Edgar Hoover's FBI got word of what the military was up to in terms of studying psychic realms and wanted to get the lowdown on what was afoot. Hoover learned, as a result of having his agents quietly approach trusted sources in the Pentagon that the U.S. Air Force had a contract in 1958 and 1959 with the Bureau of Social Science Research, which was based in Washington, D.C. The nature of that contract revolved primarily around research into hypnosis and brainwashing. Hoover was also told, however, that a part of the project concerned extra-sensory perception (ESP) and psychic phenomena. Then, from the early 1970s to the mid-1990s, the CIA, Defense Intelligence Agency, and U.S. Army all undertook extensive research into the field of psychically spying on potential enemy nations—or remote-viewing, as it is better known.

As amazing as it may sound, all of the above has now been confirmed under the terms of the Freedom of Information Act. There is, however, one program that, from the late 1960s and until at least 1972, dug deep into the arena of paranormal phenomena that few government insiders want to talk about. Even fewer want to release documents on the program. The name of the project was Operation Often, the staff of which negotiated ominous and paranormal pathways on a day-to-day basis, all thanks to the far out mind of a man named Sydney Gottlieb.

SORCERERS, SATANISM, AND THE CIA

A brilliant character that entered this world in 1918, Sydney Gottlieb was spared military service during the Second World War as a result of having been born with a club foot. Gottlieb didn't sit around feeling sorry about his circumstances and situation, however. Instead, he worked hard and secured a PhD in chemistry and a master's degree in speech therapy, the latter prompted by his own success in overcoming a major stutter that surfaced in his childhood years. But it was that PhD that opened certain secret doors for Gottlieb.

In 1951, at the age of 32, Gottlieb accepted the prestigious position of head of the Chemical division of the CIA's Technical Services Staff (TSS). It was, without doubt, a controversial job, which focused on even more controversial work: (a) studying, creating, and synthesizing fatal poisons for use in assassinations that could be made to look like death by wholly natural causes, and (b) understanding how the brain could be harnessed and controlled to create real-life Manchurian Candidates, or hypnotically controlled killers. LSD and a dizzying array of other psychoactive cocktails were very much Gottlieb's controversial tools of trade when it came to mind manipulation. It was hardly surprising, therefore, that from his colleagues at the CIA, Gottlieb acquired the memorable nickname of the Black Sorcerer. Work continued for Gottlieb into the

In the early 1970s, the CIA's Operation Often secretly studied the world of witchcraft. ©Martin Le France

two areas described above until the mid-1960s, when yet another door was opened for him. Some might say, and perhaps with a fair degree of justification, it was a doorway to the heart of Hell itself.

THE BIRTH OF OPERATION OFTEN

In late 1968, Gottlieb, having developed a keen and obsessive interest in what could justifiably be termed the black arts, made an approach to one Richard Helms, who held the position of the director of the CIA from June 1966 to February 1973. Gottlieb laid out for Helms a truly amazingly alternative idea for an ambitious project he wished to realize. It was a project aimed at digging deep into everything from black magic to voodoo, Ouija boards to séances, and devil worship to sacrificial rites. Operation Often was going to harness the forces of darkness. The reason: to try to use paranormal phenomena as a tool to psychically spy on the governments, military bodies, and intelligence agencies of potentially hostile nations, including the former Soviet Union and the People's Republic of China.

Fortunately for Gottlieb, CIA Director Helms was a man much enthused by out-of-the-box ideas. In fact, for Helms, the more out of the box those ideas were the better. Helms quickly arranged for Gottlieb to be provided with initial funding in the order of $150,000, which was a tidy sum nearly 50 years ago. Operation Often was no longer just an idea in Gottlieb's head; it was now up and running in fine, albeit controversial and supernatural fashion. But what about that name Operation Often? It hardly sounds like the sort of thing befitting a program devoted to the study of all things supernatural and devilish. Actually, it was derived from two of Gottlieb's favorite phrases, ones which he regularly used in conversation with colleagues in the intelligence arena: "...*often* we are very close to our goals then we pull back" and "...*often* we forget that the only scientific way forward is to learn from the past" (Thomas, 1988).

A great deal of Gottlieb's research that led to the establishment of Operation Often was prompted by the studies of Dr. Donald Ewen Cameron. Having graduated from the Scotland-based University of Glasgow in 1924, Cameron chose a new life for himself in Albany, New York. He, too, became a part of the CIA's secret, Cold War–era programs designed to understand and control the human mind. After Cameron's death in 1967, Gottlieb was give carte-blanche access to his files on mind manipulation. And it was while carefully scrutinizing Cameron's files that Gottlieb came to a stunning realization. Cameron, said investigative writer Gordon Thomas, was "on the verge of a breakthrough in exploring the paranormal." Far more than just mindful of this breakthrough, Gottlieb's Operation Often, said Thomas: "...was intended to take over the unfinished work, and go beyond—to explore the world of black magic and the supernatural" (Ibid.). It most definitely did exactly that, and then some.

CLAIRVOYANTS, WITCHES, AND ASTROLOGERS

One imagines the CIA filled to the brim with suave, dapper-dressed, martini-drinking spies racing around the world, wiping out the bad guys, and then celebrating by bedding an impressive bevy of bikini-clad girls. Operation Often, however, was filled with very different people: Fortune-tellers, experts in demonology, clairvoyants, and palmists were just some of the notable characters with whom its team of personnel mixed on a daily basis. Only a couple of years after it was created, Operation Often even had a trio of astrologers on board, each of who received a generous sum of $1,400 per month, plus all of their expenses. It was their particular job to carefully study newspapers and magazines for anything of a national security nature to which they might specifically be psychically alerted.

As for trying to develop a better understanding of demonology and how the forces of evil could be harnessed and utilized, in April 1972, a pair of Operation Often agents made a tactful and quiet approach to the monsignor in charge of exorcisms for New York's Catholic diocese. His response was neither tactful nor quiet. The monsignor loudly refused to have anything whatsoever to do with the program, no doubt concerned that the government was planning on trying to initiate some sort of terrible, Faustian-like pact with Satan himself—which may well have been the intention of Gottlieb and his paranormal program.

Also in April 1972, a pair of Operation Often employees made an equally quiet approach to a woman named Sybil Leek, who the BBC has since described as Britain's most famous witch. She was also the owner of a highly intelligent, but somewhat sinister, pet bird: a crow that went by the title of Mr. Hotfoot Jackson. The plan, this time, was to determine if witchcraft—and particularly the casting of malignant spells—could be used to defeat the United States' most powerful foes. But why was Leek selected, at the expense of countless other witches and warlocks? The definitive answer eludes us. It may, however, have been prompted by Leek's earlier involvement in the classified world of warfare and witchcraft.

In 1942, 30 years before she was brought on board by Operation Often, Leek was similarly secretly recruited by the British government, which demonstrates that Aleister Crowley was not the only occultist on officialdom's secret payroll in those fraught, war-torn years. It was an ingenious project in which Leek created bogus horoscopes that were then fed to the astrology-obsessed minions of Adolf Hitler. The plan was to try to destabilize those who were closer to the Fuehrer by having them believe that Leek had seen death and destruction in their immediate futures, something that might have prompted them to jump ship and help bring down the Nazi regime. Because Leek was perceived as a valuable asset to the British in the 1940s, it seems safe to say that she was seen as being precisely likewise to Operation Often by the turn of the 1970s.

NEITHER CONFIRMING NOR DENYING

The CIA admits to having files—extensive files, too—on both Sydney Gottlieb and Dr. Donald Ewen Cameron. And many of those same files are withheld for reasons having a bearing upon U.S. national security. Chiefly, they cover the 1950s, when the CIA's notorious mind-control program, MKUltra,

Demons and devils were the subject of scrutiny for Operation Often. ©Martin Schongauer

was at its height. As far as the Operation Often years are specifically concerned, however, the CIA has said little, aside from noting that documents on the Sybil Leek affair have not been located, and that papers on the brief exchange between the monsignor in charge of exorcisms for New York's Catholic diocese and personnel from Operation Often cannot be found in its archives. Even the very existence of the project itself is something the CIA cannot bring itself to admit. Interestingly, the CIA does not deny the existence of the project, either. Rather, it prefers to say not much at all, which essentially means the program *did* exist, and documentation *does* exist, but there's no chance of it ever being declassified, so go away and leave us alone. And that's as often as possible.

Operation Often aside, Richard Helms and Sydney Gottlieb popped up in yet another caper that ultimately became focused upon files that are most assuredly outside of the public arena. They are secret files that ended up torched.

11: AN ULTRA-CONTROVERSIAL PROJECT

Within the annals of research into conspiracy theories, there is perhaps no more emotive term than that of mind control. Certainly, mention those words to anyone who is even remotely aware of them and they will invariably and inevitably (and maybe justifiably) provoke imagery and comments pertaining to political assassinations, and dark and disturbing official chicanery. The specter of mind control is one that has firmly worked its ominous way into numerous facets of modern society. And it has been doing so for years. Consider, for example, the following.

"I can hypnotize a man, without his knowledge or consent, into committing treason against the United States," asserted Dr. George Estabrooks, PhD, and the chairman of the department of psychology at Colgate University, way back in 1942, and before a select group of personnel attached to the United States' War Department. Estabrooks added: "Two hundred trained foreign operators, working in the United States, could develop a uniquely dangerous army of hypnotically controlled Sixth Columnists" (Smith, 1998).

Having come to appreciate the potential military applications that mind control and hypnosis offered, when the carnage and chaos of the Second World War was over, the U.S. government decided to do something about it. In the immediate post-war period, numerous programs and projects were created by the CIA, as well as by the U.S. Navy, Army, and Air Force, to understand, harness, and control the human mind. Certainly, the most notorious of all those many and varied operations was one that began in the early 1950s. It became known as Project MKUltra, and fell under the control of the CIA. One of the most interesting things about MKUltra is that when knowledge of its secret existence began to reach Congress and the media years later—in the 1970s—senior CIA personnel raced to destroy as much of the then-still-existing documentation on the project as possible. The reason for getting rid of the files, en masse, was as simple as it was controversial: to ensure that the full story of how MKUltra had used and abused American citizens in its *Manchurian Candidate*-type operations could never be uncovered and revealed to the media and the general public. Fortunately, even the CIA was not infallible and, as a result, some files survived the destruction order, thus providing a unique and shocking look at the strange world of government-sponsored mind control at the height of the Cold War.

THE MIND GAMES BEGIN

To understand why the CIA sought to destroy as many of its MKUltra files as possible, it's important to note the scope and nature of the project. We can ascertain that much, at least, from studying those select papers that fortunately survived the destruction order. So, it is to them that we go first. Then, we will head into equally controversial territory relative to the CIA's attempts to erase significant portions of its brain-manipulating work from the history books.

It was on April 13, 1953, that MKUltra was officially, albeit secretly, approved by the CIA. Its goals were, to say the least, extremely grim. They included creating "substances which will promote illogical thinking and impulsiveness to the point where the recipient would be discredited in public"; "materials and physical methods which will produce amnesia for events preceding and during their use"; "physical methods of producing shock and confusion over extended periods of time and capable of surreptitious use"; "substances which produce physical disablement such as paralysis of the legs, acute anemia"; "a knockout pill which can surreptitiously be administered in drinks, food, cigarettes, as an aerosol, etc., which will be safe to use, provide a maximum of amnesia, and be suitable for use by agent types on an ad hoc basis"; and "a material which can be surreptitiously administered by the above routes and which in very small amounts will make it impossible for a man to perform any physical activity whatsoever" (Senate Select Committee, 1977).

On top of that, and in the first 10 years of the existence of the project, MKUltra staff immersed themselves in the study of such avenues as "radiation, electroshock, various fields of psychology, psychiatry, sociology, and anthropology, graphology, harassment substances, and paramilitary devices and

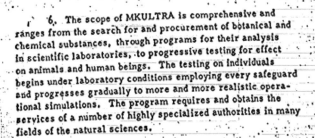

6. The scope of MKULTRA is comprehensive and ranges from the search for and procurement of botanical and chemical substances, through programs for their analysis in scientific laboratories, to progressive testing for effect on animals and human beings. The testing on individuals begins under laboratory conditions employing every safeguard and progresses gradually to more and more realistic operational simulations. The program requires and obtains the services of a number of highly specialized authorities in many fields of the natural sciences.

7. The concepts involved in manipulating human behavior are found by many people both within and outside the Agency to be distasteful and unethical. There is considerable evidence that opposition intelligence services are active and highly proficient in this field. The experience of TSD to date indicates that both the research and the employment of the materials are expensive and often unpredictable in results. Nevertheless, there have been major accomplishments both in research and operational employment.

8. The principal conclusions of the inspection are that the structure and operational controls over this activity need strengthening; improvements are needed in the administration of the research projects; and some of the testing of substances under simulated operational conditions was judged to involve excessive risk to the Agency.

9. Attached for the signature of the Deputy Director of Central Intelligence is a memorandum transmitting the report to the Deputy Director/Plans requesting a summary of action taken or comments on the recommendations contained therein.

J. G. Earman
Inspector General

Attachments - as stated

- 2 -

MKUltra: a mind-manipulating program. ©CIA, 1953

materials." The research and development of materials to be used for altering human behavior consisted of three phases: first, the search for materials suitable for study; second, laboratory testing on "voluntary" human subjects in various types of institutions; and third, the application of MKUltra materials in what were intriguingly termed "normal life settings" (Ibid.).

One of the first of the many studies conducted by the CIA was done so under the auspices of the National Institute of Mental Health. This particular program, which fell under the MKUltra banner, was intended to test a wide variety of drugs, including hallucinogenic mind-altering substances, at the NIMH Addiction Research Center in Lexington, Kentucky. The Lexington Rehabilitation Center, as it was then called, was a prison for drug addicts serving sentences for drug violations. The test subjects were volunteer prisoners who, after taking a brief physical examination and signing a general consent form, were administered hallucinogenic drugs. As a reward for their participation in the program, the addicts were provided with welcome amounts of the drug (or drugs) of their personal choice.

It was out of this program that the fertile seeds of mind control were soon sown. Those seeds later bloomed, and duly blossomed, into a wealth of subprojects that, rumor has it, delved into major controversial issues. They are said to have included (a) the creation of programmed assassins, those people controlled and directed via a combination of chemicals and deep hypnosis techniques to commit murder as shadowy forces saw fit; (b) the use of psychedelics and mind-altering technology to create bogus alien abduction events, the reason being to determine how effectively the CIA could make unwitting citizens see just about anything the agency wanted them to see; and (c) the outright sacrifice of American lives to further the cause of mind control research during the Cold War.

AT THE HELM OF DESTRUCTION

In late 1972, Richard Helms, who held the position of CIA director from June 1966 to February 1973, learned to his consternation that certain people within the U.S. media had been given snippets of data on the ins and outs of MKUltra. The source of the leaks was never identified or proved, but Helms considered that the leaks possibly came from within the heart of the agency itself. Realizing quickly and astutely that any mainstream media exposure of the story pertaining to, and the work of, MKUltra could prove disastrous, Helms knew there was no alternative but to ensure that as many of the MKUltra

(d) What are the present capabilities and limitations of the substance for clandesinte operations?

(e) What further research is being conducted on this and related substances and how does this reflect existing TSD capabilities, operational requirements and budget factors?

(3) MKULTRA records afforded no such approach to inspection. There are just two individuals in TSD who have full substantive knowledge of the program and most of that knowledge is unrecorded. Both are highly skilled, highly motivated, professionally compstent individuals. Part of their competence lies in their command of intelligence tradecraft. In protecting the sensitive nature of the American intelligence capability to manipulate human behavior, they apply "need to know" doctrine to their professional associates and to their clerical assistants to a maximum degree. Confidence in their competence and discretion has been a vital feature of the management of MKULTRA.

c. Advanced testing of MKULTRA materials:

It is the firm doctrine in TSD that testing of materials under accepted scientific procedures fails to disclose the full pattern of reactions and attributions that may occur

- 6 -

Controlling the mind, MKUltra-style. ©CIA, 1953

documents as possible never saw the light of day. To many people, this might seem strange. After all, Helms was ordering the obliteration of literally tens of thousands of pages of historical material on a project of undeniably ground-breaking proportions. But there's an important reason why Helms's decision made complete sense to both him and to those within the CIA working in the mind-control arena.

By 1972, the decades-old files in question were certainly of historical significance, as they told and revealed the scope of the program, as well as some of the controversial things that had been done in the name of national security back in the early to mid-1950s. Their continued existence in 1972, however, wasn't seen as necessarily being crucial to the CIA. By the early 1970s, the research and development work was long over, the programs were all up and running in stealth, and there was no need to commit anything to paper anymore. So, destroying the original research material spawned in the 1950s bothered Helms not a bit. In fact, trashing the whole lot would serve a very good purpose, from Helms's position. It would help prevent the secrets surrounding the extent to which mind-control programs were part and parcel of everyday life at the CIA from falling into what Helms saw as being the wrong hands.

Acting on the secret orders of Richard Helms, Sidney Gottlieb was the man tasked with destroying the CIA's MKUltra document collection. Gottlieb, as we saw in the previous chapter, was one of the key players in yet another controversial CIA-created project that remains largely hidden behind closed doors, namely the occult-dominated Operation Often.

GOTTLIEB BURNS...AND BURNS... AND BURNS...

The overwhelming majority of the CIA's records on MKUltra were held tightly at its records facility, which was located in Warrenton, Virginia, less than a one-hour drive from the agency's headquarters at Langley. It was on the morning of January 30, 1973, that Sidney Gottlieb made the drive that led to the snuffing out of a significant part of the CIA's history. On the previous day, Helms's office had advised the director of the records facility of what would be going down only 24 hours later. The latter was far from being a happy man, and he expressed his concerns to Gottlieb on the morning in question that the large-scale burning of boxes and boxes of official material was way out of order. Gottlieb merely waved him aside, stating that if he had a problem he should take it up with Director Helms, on whose direct orders Gottlieb was himself acting. The man did exactly that and also prepared a statement for Helms's attention, chiefly to protect him from accusations of any claims of wrong-doing.

It was a statement that survived the destruction notice and clearly noted the objections made to Gottlieb. The poor man could only look on helplessly. With appalled frustration he watched as Gottlieb oversaw the fiery destruction—by colleagues from the CIA's Technical Services Division—of decades of priceless files.

Gottlieb wasn't done, however. In fact, he had just gotten started. To protect himself from potential prosecution if any evidence surfaced suggesting he had crossed the line and broken the law in terms of his own involvement in MKUltra, Gottlieb did something else. He ordered his chief assistant to relegate to cinders all papers on the project contained in his, Gottlieb's, own office. She dutifully followed her orders. Then, in December 1974, the nightmarish scenario that both Helms and Gottlieb anticipated became grim reality. The *New York Times* ran a prominent article from Pulitzer prize–winning journalist, Seymour Hersh that made mention of MKUltra, as well as its mind control theme. The floodgates were about to open wide and a deluge of secrets was ready and waiting to cascade forth.

THE U.S. SENATE TAKES NOTE

Not long after Seymour Hersh's *New York Times* article appeared, an official investigation of MKUltra began. It was coordinated by the U.S. Senate Select Committee to Study Governmental Operations with Respect to Intelligence Activities (the Church Committee, as it was also known, as a result of it being chaired by Senator Frank Church) and the United States President's Commission on CIA activities within the United States (more popularly referred to as the Rockefeller Commission, after Vice President Nelson Rockefeller). This investigation was undertaken to determine if, during Operation MKUltra (a) the CIA had engaged in illegal activity, (b) the personal rights of citizens had been violated, and (c) the project at issue had resulted in any deaths—which assuredly and unfortunately it did.

The story that unfolded was both dark and disturbing, in equal, stark degrees. Indeed, the scope of the project—and allied operations—was spelled out in an August 1977 document titled *The Senate MKUltra Hearings* that was prepared by the Senate Select Committee on Intelligence and the Committee on Human Resources, as a result of its probing into the secret world of the CIA. The authors of the document explained:

> *Research and development programs to find materials which could be used to alter human behavior were initiated in the late 1940s and early 1950s. These experimental programs originally included testing of drugs*

involving witting human subjects, and culminated in tests using unwitting, non-volunteer human subjects. These tests were designed to determine the potential effects of chemical or biological agents when used operationally against individuals unaware that they had received a drug (Senate Select Committee, 1977).

The committee then turned its attention to the overwhelming secrecy that surrounded these early 1940s/1950s projects, noting that: "The highly compartmented nature of these programs may be explained in part by an observation made by the CIA Inspector General that, 'the knowledge that the Agency is engaging in unethical and illicit activities would have serious repercussions in political and diplomatic circles and would be detrimental to the accomplishment of its missions'" (Ibid.).

The committee starkly noted: "While some controlled testing of these substances might be defended, the nature of the tests, their scale, and the fact that they were continued for years after the danger of surreptitious administration of LSD to unwitting individuals was known, demonstrate a fundamental disregard for the value of human life" (Ibid.).

In conclusion, it's important to note that the committee's 1975 findings and observations on the CIA's MKUltra program were filled with tales of flagrant disregard for human rights and human safety. But there's something else: Those same findings and observations were based upon an evaluation of the papers that survived the attempts of Helms and Gottlieb to destroy the entire MKUltra archive. Can you imagine how much more inflammatory the committee's conclusions could have been if they had also been given access to those boxes upon boxes that ended up burned to a crisp two years earlier? Unfortunately, it's almost certain that we'll never know the full nature and scope of the papers that Helms and Gottlieb decided were for nobody's eyes only—and that included the highest echelons of the U.S. Senate.

The story of ream after ream of files being burned is not over, however. Nor is the saga of MKUltra. Both issues played significant roles in a still-unexplained fire that laid waste to a certain government facility, and millions of pages of documents, only five months after Richard Helms stepped down as the director of the CIA.

12: FANNING THE FLAMES OF CONSPIRACY

Shortly after the witching hour on July 12, 1973, a catastrophic fire broke out at one of the most important facilities of the United States government. Fortunately, no lives were lost in the inferno. But something else was lost, and on a truly massive scale: numerous military personnel records, specifically relative to American citizens who had served in the Army and the Air Force between 1912 and 1964. Although the official verdict is that the fire was not the result of a deliberate act, whispers that full blown arson was afoot continue to circulate decades later. They are whispers that, when we carefully follow the winding trail, take us right back to the controversial world of the CIA's MKUltra program. As we have seen, that, too, was a matter dominated by the wholesale destruction of official files on a massive scale—and also, as it transpires, by fire. Before we get to the matter of a certain conspiracy theory that surrounds the entire affair, however, let's have a careful look at what actually happened on that blazing, hot night, and what officialdom has to say about the event—officially, at least.

The building that suffered so much damage, and which has since provoked so much intrigue, fell under the auspices of the National Personnel Records Center (NPRC). Created in 1956, the NPRC is an agency of the National Archives and Records Administration and is the primary storage area for the official records of all men and women in the United States who have served their country in the military or at a civilian, governmental level. The records on the former are held at the Military Personnel Records Center, and files on the latter are found at the Civilian Personnel Records Center, both in St. Louis, Missouri. And it is to the Military Personnel Records Center that we have to now turn our attention.

The building itself was designed by Minoru Yamasaki, a brilliant American architect who was also the brains behind the World Trade Center's Twin Towers, which came crashing down on September 11, 2001, an event that is also surrounded by a wealth of conspiracy theories. It was in 1951 that the Department of Defense approached Yamasaki with the offer to design, and ultimately oversee the building of, the new facility. Yamasaki was eager to get on board. Since the building was due to house millions of pages of official records, the DoD arranged for Yamasaki to visit certain already-existing government archives, including the New York–based U.S. Navy Records Center, which had a first class fire-prevention system in place. Yamasaki was also given a tour of a Pentagon-run installation in Virginia that lacked any provisions, at all, for coping with a fire, large or small.

More than a bit puzzled, Yamasaki asked why such glaring differences existed between two government-controlled locations, both tasked with record-keeping. The answer was that archivists were in conflict regarding what could cause most damage to important documents: an actual fire, or a building-wide water sprinkler system that, when activated, might well end up destroying far more papers than any theoretical fire ever could. So, it was explained to Yamasaki, some archives had in-built means to deal with a fire, whereas others—in a worst case scenario—would have to wait for local fire trucks to arrive. As a result, the Military Personnel Records Center (MPRC) was constructed without the benefit of any means to combat a serious fire in the slightest. It was a decision that, as history has demonstrated, proved to be extremely costly. The overall construction of the MPRC was completed by 1956. It was an impressive facility: More than 1,200,000 square-feet, spread across six floors, served as a collective storage area for millions of pages of official documentation. Everything ran smoothly and safely until that fateful night in the summer of 1973.

PHONES RING WHILE A BUILDING BURNS

The first indication that something serious was happening came just after 12:15 a.m., when the fire department of Olivette, a suburb of St. Louis, received a panicky phone call stating that the records center was ablaze. Only a minute or so later, a security guard—on duty at ground-floor level—got a call from a motorcyclist who, while driving past the building, saw flames coming from the top floor. Full credit to the fire service; they were on the scene by 12:20 a.m. That the fire was on the sixth floor of the building, however, ensured that it quickly spread before firefighters had the opportunity to prevent major damage from occurring. In fact, the fire didn't just spread; it got totally out of control. For three hours, practically all of St. Louis' firefighters did their best to extinguish the blaze but, in the end, it was to no avail. Shortly after 3:00 a.m., and as a result of the intense heat and billowing smoke, the firefighters were forced to make a retreat. Attempts were made to put the fire out by saturating the outer walls of the building with water, and directing hosepipes at broken windows, hoping that this might at least extinguish some of the flames. The operation was not overly successful, however, and the fire raged on for no less than three days. Not only that, it was actually four and a half days before local fire chiefs felt comfortable in confirming that the fire was completely out, and that there was no chance of it reigniting anywhere in those parts of the building that were untouched by the inferno.

The loss of records was devastating: Somewhere between 16 and 18 million files on U.S. military personnel were gone, burned to nothingness. Worse still, no copies of the documents—whether in the form of photocopies or microfilm—had ever been made, in the event that such a catastrophe occurred. In other words, the files were really gone; as was the sixth floor, which was ruined by the blaze. This was, in the minds of some, a disaster just waiting to happen. After all, there was no meaningful fire-prevention equipment in the building—a building that just happened to be filled to the brim with paper. And, as the facility staff attested, during the hot summer months in St. Louis, and particularly in those parts of the building where ventilation and air-conditioning were kept at a minimum to ensure that degradation to the papers did not occur, that same paper got undeniably warm. Not unreasonably, some wondered if, perhaps, that had led to spontaneous combustion and ensuing, irreversible disaster. That cigarette butts were found, by FBI agents, in several trashcans in the building made some investigators of the fire wonder if sheer carelessness was the cause of the destruction. The official verdict, however, was that the circumstances that led to the fire could not be fully explained. There was no proof of spontaneous combustion caused by piles of paper getting steadily warmer. Nor was there any hard evidence to suggest that a reckless smoker was the cause of the destruction. Everything was circumstantial and theory-driven. And talking of theories for the fire, there is another one. It takes us back to the controversial world of the CIA, mind control, and MKUltra.

ANONYMOUS LETTERS AND ALIENS THAT APPARENTLY WEREN'T ALIENS

In the summer of 1971, the FBI received a strangely worded, unsigned, typed letter. It can now be viewed, online, at the Bureau's Vault Website and reads as follows:

> *In approximately seven months or January 1972, certain copies of top-secret documents shall be sent to the* New York Times *as well as to two other newspapers. These documents are related to and will be an ostentation [sic] of the involvement of the Pentagon in the controversial 'Unidentified Flying Objects' or 'Flying Saucer' subject. It will show that not only the US Air Force was involved in UFO research but the other military branches as well ("UFO," 2013).*

> *Analysis and the actual conclusions of the classic UFO cases shall be revealed. This shall be accomplished by zeroxed [sic] documents and photographs that General Wolfe had received when he was head of the Army's UFO support program in the Pentagon during the Eisenhower years (Ibid.).*

> *Sorry, but it is concluded here that this is the best course to take because we feel that the secret UFO investigations are parallel in nature to the Times-Pentagon-Vietnam controversy. If we are wrong in taking this action, time will tell (Ibid.).*

Approximately two months later, a further piece of correspondence on this matter reached the FBI. It had the same postmark, and the handwriting on the envelope was the same. The second letter elaborated on the first, but with an interesting, and perhaps to the FBI, unforeseen, twist. The story that the secret files would reveal, claimed the unknown writer, was that many famous UFO encounters and incidents involving presumed alien entities were, in reality, nothing of the sort. The writer maintained that the records that had been acquired showed how the CIA's mind control projects had manipulated an unidentified number of U.S. citizens into believing they had undergone flying saucer encounters. In reality, said the anonymous writer, the witnesses were the victims of sophisticated mind alteration. Adding even more to the controversy was the assertion that some of those people included American servicemen and women that had volunteered to take part in the secret operations. The inference was that those same service personnel were used in mind-altering programs to gauge the extent to which alien-like experiences could be fabricated by rendering the targeted individuals into chemically altered states. Equally intriguing, the letter writer made it clear that verification of the identities of the Army and Air Force employees in question—who would play a role in informing the *New York Times* of the controversial facts—would be made from historical papers held at the National Personnel Records Center.

There is strong evidence that the CIA's MKUltra program did indeed explore the issue of using hallucinogenic substances as a means to fabricate UFO events—chiefly, it seems, to blur the truth about what was, and perhaps still is, at the heart of the UFO mys-

CIA Director Richard Helms, the man behind the destruction of the MKUltra documents. ©CIA, 1969

tery. In my *Contactees* book, for example, I presented data on more than a few individuals in 1950s era UFO research that appeared to have been drugged by government agents in relation to certain UFO events. One of those was a man named Orfeo Angelucci, who claimed face-to-face encounters with suspiciously human-looking extraterrestrials in California in 1952. On one occasion, in a desert-based diner outside of Los Angeles, Angelucci was prompted by a strange and enigmatic visitor in black to swallow a small pill, which, unfathomably and recklessly, Angelucci did, and without giving the matter barely a second thought. Within half an hour, he was experiencing profound visionary experiences that strongly suggested he had been hit by something akin to LSD. As Angelucci's mind expanded, his mouth went into overtime, and he spouted for hours to the man in black on the nature of his alleged alien encounters, what they meant to him, where the other-worldly visitors came from, and their intent. All the time, Angelucci said, years later, a pair of uniformed military personnel watched him closely from the opposite table—no doubt, fully approving of the way in which MKUltra's techniques had the man convinced he had met with aliens from a world far away, but that actually never existed.

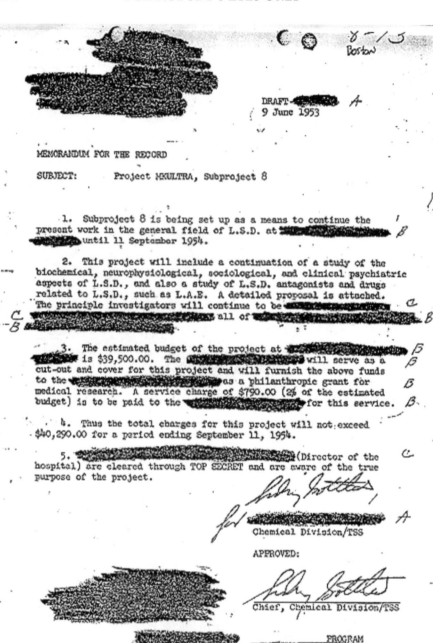

DRAFT- A
9 June 1953

MEMORANDUM FOR THE RECORD

SUBJECT: Project MKULTRA, Subproject 8

   1. Subproject 8 is being set up as a means to continue the
present work in the general field of L.S.D. at
until 11 September 1954.

   2. This project will include a continuation of a study of the
biochemical, neurophysiological, sociological, and clinical psychiatric
aspects of L.S.D., and also a study of L.S.D. antagonists and drugs
related to L.S.D., such as L.A.E. A detailed proposal is attached.
The principle investigators will continue to be
all of

   3. The estimated budget of the project at
is $39,500.00. The   will serve as a
cut-out and cover for this project and will furnish the above funds
to the   as a philanthropic grant for
medical research. A service charge of $790.00 (2% of the estimated
budget) is to be paid to the   for this service.

   4. Thus the total charges for this project will not exceed
$40,290.00 for a period ending September 11, 1954.

   5.   (Director of the
hospital) are cleared through TOP SECRET and are aware of the true
purpose of the project.

Chemical Division/TSS

APPROVED:

Chief, Chemical Division/TSS

PROGRAM

In the 1950s, research into LSD was at the forefront of the work of MKUltra. ©CIA, 1953

BURNING THE EVIDENCE

There's no doubt that the two letters sent to the FBI told the fragments of an amazing story, but one that sounds not so far out, given what we know about the groundbreaking research and results of MKUltra. Some might suggest that such outlandish claims should be dismissed out of hand, particularly because the writer was careful to protect his or her identity. But we should perhaps not rush to judgment. It's intriguing that the person behind the letters claimed the secret files—which had the CIA's mind control research at its heart—would be sent to the *New York Times*. As noted in the previous chapter, it was indeed the *New York Times* that broke the MKUltra story in December 1974, when Pulitzer Prize–winning journalist, Seymour Hersh made mention of MKUltra, as well as its mind-manipulating goals.

As we have seen, when fears surfaced within the CIA that outside digging threatened to reveal to the world at large the true scope of MKUltra, the agency's director, Richard Helms—along with Sydney Gottlieb—arranged for the almost complete destruction of the MKUltra archive. Remember how the destruction was achieved: by relegating the files to a furnace, in January 1973, at the CIA's records facility, which was located in Warrenton, Virginia. Why is this important? Because the FBI's anonymous letter writer claimed that the names of the military personnel involved in this UFO/mind control operation could be verified by checking the files held at the National Personnel Records Center's facility in St. Louis. That is, they could be checked until July 1973, when millions of pages of such records conveniently went up in smoke.

How curious that certain interconnected files relative to this same story—namely, those related to mind control, those documents that fell under the control of CIA director Helms, and those that were housed in the Military Personnel Records Center—all ended up burned to a crisp, the former on the secret orders of Helms, and the latter as a result of a still-unexplained fire. That the massively destructive fire at the MPRC took place only a handful of months after Sydney Gottlieb tossed tens of thousands of pages of MKUltra material into a fiery furnace only makes matters even more intriguing when it comes to addressing the contents of those anonymous letters sent to the FBI. As does the fact that the FBI's informant had made a direct connection between the documentation on mind-manipulation techniques and the papers held at the records center.

History has shown that, although files on about 18 million Americans were forever lost in that destructive fire, about 34 million dossiers survived the blaze. But that was only as a result of the incredibly swift arrival of the local fire service. Had they not been on the scene in mere minutes, the loss could have been total. Moreover, those files that were destroyed included biographical data on (a) more than 75 percent of all U.S. Air Force personnel whose service spanned 1947 to 1960 and whose surnames ran from H to Z, and (b) more than 80 percent of U.S. Army employees whose terms of employment ran up to 1960. Notably, 1947 to the early 1960s was the period when mind control research was at its height within the CIA. After that period, pretty much everything had been perfected, and the early research material was no longer needed—hence why Richard Helms had no qualms about destroying the many pages of data that told the shocking story of MKUltra's earliest years.

Could it have been the case that there were certain figures in government, or within the domain of intelligence work, who felt that simply getting rid of the MKUltra files was not enough? Given the nature of the letters sent to the FBI—copies of which were shared with both the Pentagon and the CIA—is it possible that someone, somewhere, deliberately engineered the disastrous fire at the Military Personnel Records Center? If so, might such an operation have been initiated to try to prevent outside digging into the lives and careers of some of those military personnel who knew of the deeper and weirder UFO-related aspects of MKUltra, and of the clear abuses of power and violation of citizens who became guinea pigs in the operation?

And, still on the subject of guinea pigs, let us see what happens when people with power use it against the weak and the vulnerable, all in the name of medical advancement.

13: EXPERIMENTS ON HUMANS

On June 12, 2001, Western Australia Newspapers Ltd. revealed the astounding details of a deeply controversial story that, surely, no one wished to be true. But it may well have been precisely that. It was a disturbing and dark tale that told of shocking and secret experiments undertaken by military personnel on physically handicapped individuals during the early years of the Cold War. As the newspaper noted, an untold number of people with serious physical and mental disabilities were used as human guinea pigs at the height of British nuclear tests. The tests were undertaken, during the 1950s, at Australia's Maralinga Test Site. Between 1955 and 1963, Maralinga—which is a part of the Woomera Test Range, falls under the jurisdiction of the Royal Australian Air Force, and is situated in South Australia—served as the prime location from where the British government carried out its early atomic tests. Operation Antler and Operation Buffalo were just two of the many such operations in which thermonuclear weapons were detonated on Australian soil to determine their pulverizing effects on the landscape.

According to information brought to the attention of newspaper staff, a control group of handicapped people was clandestinely flown to the British test site as part of a classified program designed to evaluate the physical effects of exposure to high levels of radiation. As the newspaper learned, that same control group all died: Deadly fallout was the unsurprising and rapid cause. The sensational story was loudly and swiftly denounced as nonsense by the governments of both Britain and Australia. But it refused to go away. And it had notable support in high places. Dr. Robert Jackson, the director of the Center for Disability Research and Development at Edith Cowan University in Australia, decided to go public, revealing that he had heard such stories in the 1980s. One such account came from a former military man who claimed to have flown an entire plane full of handicapped people from the UK to the Maralinga site when the tests were at their height. The pilot chillingly advised Dr. Jackson, in words that do not leave much doubt about how they should be interpreted, that they didn't fly them out again.

The Australian government *did* concede, back in 1994, that local Aboriginal people known as the Maralinga Tjarutja had suffered adversely, health-wise, as a result of the tests (something that finally led to a payment of compensation in the order of $13.5 million), but no one at an official level was willing to go as far as admitting to having used handicapped people in atomic bomb tests. Nor have any official files on these specific allegations and claims ever surfaced. That does not mean the tales lack merit. How can we be so sure? Simple: They have their overseas counterparts.

In the 1990s, a huge inquiry was launched in the United States to determine the extent to which unethical, and even illegal, testing of a radiation-based nature was undertaken on human guinea pigs when the Cold War reigned. It turns out that extent was huge. It also turns out that extensive digging uncovered the intriguing fact that masses of files on these experiments had taken a hike; to where, no one in government seemingly had a clue. Either that or they weren't saying.

CLINTON CREATES A COMMITTEE

On January 15, 1994, then U.S. President Bill Clinton established what was described as the Advisory Committee on Human Radiation Experiments, or ACHRE. Its official mandate was to get to the bottom of reports, testimony, and claims to the effect that unethical medical experiments had been carried out on American citizens from, chiefly, the mid-1940s to the early 1970s. ACHRE was comprised of a wide and varied body of highly respected individuals, including 13 experts in bioethics, radiation oncology and biology, nuclear medicine, epidemiology and bio-statistics, public health, the history of science and medicine, and law.

President Clinton ordered the committee to make its conclusions and recommendations known to a newly created Cabinet-level group that was given the title of the Human Radiation Interagency Working Group. Its membership was as prestigious as it was powerful, and included the secretaries of defense, energy, health and human services, and veterans affairs; the attorney general; the administrator of the National Aeronautics and Space Administration (NASA); the director of the CIA; and the director of the Office of Management and Budget.

The very existence of the experiments under scrutiny provoked a number of important and challenging questions: How many experiments were conducted or sponsored by government agencies, and why? How many were kept hidden? Was anyone—deliberately or otherwise—harmed or possibly even killed as a result of the experimentation? What, if anything at all, was disclosed to those who were subjected to risk? What opportunity, if

In 1994, President Bill Clinton authorized an investigation of radiation-based experiments undertaken on U.S. citizens between 1944 and 1972. ©U.S. government, 1993

any, did they have to give their consent? By what rules should the actions of those who masterminded the decades-old projects be judged today, if at all? What remedies were due to those who were wronged, harmed, or killed by such experimentation? To what extent did legislation exist to ensure nothing of a similar nature was still going on at the time of the inquiry? And, finally, what could be learned, ethically, morally, and scientifically, from addressing the scope of the experimentation? President Clinton made it clear he wanted answers. And he wanted them quickly. He got them, but they may not have been all that he was anticipating and hoping for.

RADIATION FILES: LOST AND DESTROYED

The reason why ACHRE focused, specifically, on the years 1944 to 1974 was a logical one. The first was the earliest date upon which evidence was uncovered related to a radiation-themed experiment having been undertaken on an American citizen, on U.S. soil. The latter date was the year in which the Department of Health, Education and Welfare created new rules to try to ensure that no one in officialdom ever again overstepped the mark in terms of the moral and ethical aspects of human testing. With the assistance of hundreds of federal officials, the committee located and carefully studied literally hundreds of thousands of government documents, many running to hundreds of pages, and the vast majority of them classified Secret or Top Secret. But there was something else, too—something we have seen time and again in the pages of this book.

According to ACHRE staff, even though internal references contained in some of the Top Secret files alluded to even more, and perhaps controversial, programs that utilized human guinea pigs in the testing of nuclear materials, a number of these files could not be found, or had been destroyed decades earlier. It's important, too, that ACHRE could not resolve the matter of *how* or *why* some of the files came to be lost or destroyed. Certainly, no documentation giving orders for the destruction of immense file collections was ever found. And no explanation was provided for how what was estimated to be tens of thousands of additional files could end up missing.

Nevertheless, the documents that *were* found, even if they only amounted to a fragment of the full story, led to the identification of nearly 4,000 human radiation experiments secretly sponsored by agencies of government, the military, and the intelligence community from the 1940s to the 1970s. They included: experiments with plutonium and other atomic bomb materials; the Atomic Energy Commission's program of radioisotope distribution; non-therapeutic research on children, and physically and mentally handicapped people who had been secretly taken from asylums; total body irradiation; radiation research undertaken on prisoners in American jails; human experimentation in connection with nuclear weapons testing; intentional environmental releases of radiation; and even research involving health effects on uranium miners.

The experiments, the Committee explained, were conducted to advance biomedical science; some experiments were conducted to advance national interests in defense or space exploration; and others served both biomedical and defense or space exploration purposes. It was, to say the least, a jaw-dropping list. Interestingly, as the Committee noted, on the matters above, and regarding the vast majority of the files uncovered, only fragmentary evidence was available for scrutiny. Again, ACHRE could offer no viable, or justifiable, reason why that should have been the case.

That all of the above amounted to the tip of the iceberg and the rest of that iceberg had curiously sunk without a trace—either that or someone had pulled all the missing files and destroyed or hidden them years ago—made many in

Today, many of the official files on radiation tests on human subjects cannot be found. ©*U.S. government*

ACHRE wonder not so much about what they *did* uncover, but the true nature and extent of what they *didn't*. In its conclusions, ACHRE advised President Clinton and his staff that, although some observations and conclusions could be reached, the complete lack of access to certain papers that should have been found, but weren't, meant that the picture of the past—and the recommendations for the present and future—were significantly and woefully incomplete.

ACHRE noted that the Atomic Energy Commission, the Defense Department, and the National Institutes of Health all recognized, as far back as the 1940s, that research into the effects of radiation on human beings should only have pressed ahead with the consent of the subject or subjects involved, or the consent of their legal guardians or custodians. In reality, however, the committee members admitted to their concern that, very little evidence was uncovered suggesting consent had been sought of those that were exploited in the experiments. This, of course, adds much weight to the claims coming out of Australia about handicapped individuals being used and abused in nightmarish, nuclear fashion—individuals who clearly had very little to say in, or control over, the matter of how and why they were sacrificed in the name of national security, nuclear science, and medicine.

Government officials and investigators, reported ACHRE, "...are blameworthy for not having had policies and practices in place to protect the rights and interests of human subjects who were used in research from which the subjects could not possibly derive direct medical benefit" (*Advisory Committee on Radiation Experiments*, 1995).

Particularly damning was the following from ACHRE: "Information about human experiments was kept secret out of concern for embarrassment to the government, potential legal liability, and worry that public misunderstanding would jeopardize government programs. There is no evidence that issues of fairness or concerns about exploitation in the selection of subjects figured in policies or rules of the period" (Ibid.).

From medical controversies and missing medical files, we now take a trip into the mystery-filled domain of outer space.

14: A SECRET SPACE PROGRAM

For years, captivating stories have circulated that hidden very deeply and successfully within the U.S. military infrastructure is what, in simple terms, could be described as a secret space program. That's to say, a program that runs alongside the publicly visible work of NASA, the National Aeronautics and Space Administration. Whereas NASA's mandate is to explore space for scientific reasons, conspiracy theorists say that the goal of the Pentagon's project is the militarization of the vast domain beyond our world. The rumors suggest that not only does the military have a classified space program, but also secret bases on the far side of the Moon and a fleet of highly advanced, manned spacecraft that may even have clandestinely visited Mars and some of the other planets in our solar system. To be sure, it's a wild scenario that sounds like equally wild science fiction. It is, however, one that has some degree of support for it. And some of that support comes in the form of testimony from people who claim to have read files, and seen photos, that appear to strongly validate the story. Problematic is the fact that those photos and files—just like so many others discussed in previous chapters—are suspiciously missing.

One person who has spoken out on such matters is a respected historian, Richard Dolan. He notes: "Over the years I have encountered no shortage of quiet, serious-minded people who tell me of their knowledge that there is such a covert program. Are there bases on the far side of the Moon? I do not know for sure, but I cannot rule it out" (Dolan, 2010).

A SECRET BASE ON THE HORIZON

Dolan's suspicions may be absolutely on target. Less than one year after NASA was formally brought into being—July 29, 1958—the U.S. military was already planning to play an active, ambitious, and secret role in outer space. On March 20, 1959, Lieutenant General Arthur G. Trudeau, who, at the time,

was the U.S. Army's chief of research and development, put the finishing touches to a huge report that recommended the construction—at a cost of around $6 billion—of a Pentagon-controlled base on the surface of the Moon. The operation was code-named Project Horizon. In his report, Trudeau noted:

There is a requirement for a manned military outpost on the moon. The lunar outpost is required to develop and protect potential United States interests on the moon; to develop techniques in moon-based surveillance of the earth and space, in communica-

General Arthur Trudeau, who, in 1959, prepared a lengthy, secret document on the building of a military base on the Moon. ©U.S. Army

tions relay, and in operations on the surface of the moon; to serve as a base for exploration of the moon, for further exploration into space and for military operations on the moon if required; and to support scientific investigations on the moon (Trudeau, 1959).

Officially, the program was cancelled due to the limitations of technology available in the late 1950s and early 1960s. It's interesting, however, that the Army's original plan was to have the first stages of the base up and running by 1965. Why, you may well ask, is this so interesting? In that same year, 1965, photos were seen by a former U.S. Air Force operative that seemed to show just such a base on the surface of the Moon—photos that have since vanished. That man confided in a colleague, one Karl Wolfe, who, at the time, held a

Top Secret clearance. In the same year that the U.S. Army planned on having the first stages of its Moon base in place, Wolfe spent time working at Langley Air Force Base, Virginia, on a project linked to the technology surrounding NASA's lunar orbiter. While at Langley, Wolfe had the opportunity to speak with a colleague on the same project and who had an extraordinary story to tell. Highly concerned about the nature of the material to which he had been exposed, the man, seemingly, was looking for someone in whom he could confide. That man turned out to be Karl Wolfe.

As Wolfe listened carefully, an extraordinary story came tumbling out: NASA had discovered evidence of the existence of some form of lunar outpost on the far side of the Moon. Of course, 1965 was four years before *Apollo 11* landed on the Moon and Neil Armstrong became the first person to set foot on the surface of our nearest neighbor in the solar system. Clearly, almost half a decade before NASA landed men on the Moon, no one should have been in a position to do something identical, never mind construct a futuristic installation on its rocky, cratered surface. But, for all intents and purposes, that seemed to have been exactly what had been achieved. Wolfe, astutely realizing that the talkative airman was probably breaching secrecy protocols on a serious basis, quickly broke off the conversation. But he never forgot the tantalizing story of how NASA had apparently learned, to its amazement and concern, that someone had beaten them in the race to the Moon. Maybe that someone was not E.T., but Army personnel attached to a secret program born out of the plans, goals, and recommendations of Lieutenant General Arthur G. Trudeau back in 1959.

SPYING PSYCHICALLY ON A MOON BASE

In the early 1970s, various arms of American officialdom, including the Defense Intelligence Agency, CIA, and U.S. Army, began to explore the potential espionage-based profits that could be gained from something that became known as remote-viewing. In simple terms, remote-viewing, for the government, meant using the psychic abilities of the mind to spy on potential enemy powers, such as the former Soviet Union. One of the most gifted of the government's remote-viewers during this period was a man named Ingo Swann. Working alongside secretive, and sometimes sinister, government types became day-to-day routine for Swann. But certainly the most sinister of all was a character who Swann came briefly to know and who only ever referred to himself as Mr. Axelrod.

It was early in February 1975 when Swann was quietly contacted by a certain highly placed figure in Washington, D.C., who told Swann to soon expect a phone call from a man named Mr. Axelrod. Swann's source admitted that he was unable to say much else at that time, except that Mr. Axelrod's call would be one of great significance and importance. And it was made abundantly clear to Swann that he should not ignore the call. A month or so later, the call finally came through. Axelrod—if that was his real name, something that Swann doubted—made it clear that he wanted a head-to-head meeting at the Museum of Natural History at the Smithsonian. Not only that, Axelrod wanted the meeting not tomorrow, next week, or next month, but within the next few hours. A puzzled, and slightly alarmed, Swann nevertheless agreed and made his way to the Smithsonian.

Evidently, Axelrod knew what Swann looked like. While the latter walked around the Smithsonian wondering what might happen next, he was approached by a Marine-type, who told him what was going to happen next. Swann was first taken on a brief car journey to a location where a helicopter was sitting on a concreted piece of ground. On clambering aboard, he was blindfolded and flown to another location, one never disclosed to Swann, although he was able to determine that the flight lasted under 30 minutes. Whatever the nature of the installation to which Swann was taken, it was evidently impressive. While still blindfolded, Swann was taken into an elevator that, he later revealed, seemed to descend near-endlessly. Clearly, Swann was deep underground, in some secure, bunker-like construction of officialdom.

When the blindfold was finally removed, Swann could see that standing right in front of him was a well-dressed man. It was Mr. Axelrod, who finally admitted to a hardly surprised Swann that this was not his real name. Axelrod, or whoever he really was, got right to the crux of the matter. After reeling off question upon question about remote-viewing and the extent to which it was deemed successful in terms of spying and espionage-based operations, Axelrod announced that he wanted to make use of Swann's talents. And, as a thank you, Axelrod was prepared to pay, and pay very well, too. Swann, admittedly intrigued by the whole affair, quickly got on board.

Axelrod inquired of Swann what he knew about the Moon. Now, finally, the purpose of the strange get-together was becoming apparent. Someone at an official level—Swann assumed, probably correctly, that Axelrod was some sort of government spook—wanted the Moon remote-viewed, which is exactly what happened. Given what we know today about Project Horizon and the testimony of Karl Wolfe, it's decidedly notable that Swann reported to Axelrod that, while in a psychic state of mind, he could see on the Moon a number of dome-shaped buildings, machinery that seemed to be of a construction-based nature, and even mining operations. Had extraterrestrials from a far away galaxy made the Moon their home? Almost certainly not. Swann's powers also revealed the existence of a facility that was built out of, and extended deep within, a nearby cliff-face. A great deal of work was afoot within this highly advanced installation. But those

The Moon: a site of military secrets. ©NASA

manning it were not those bug-eyed little beings of the type that dominate so-called alien abduction lore in today's world and popular culture. No, they appeared to be nothing more than regular human beings, just like me and you.

Fascinated by this, Axelrod then asked Swann if he was familiar with the work of a certain George Leonard. Swann replied that no, he was not. Although Swann did not know it—but Axelrod evidently did and told Swann so—Leonard was also digging into the matter of strange structures seen on the surface of the Moon. Indeed, in 1977 Leonard's own book on this controversial topic, titled *Somebody Else Is on the Moon*, was published. Then, without a word of warning, the meeting was over. Swann was thanked for his time, paid very handsomely, and taken back to the Smithsonian—but not before, of course, having to put that blindfold back on for a mysterious return journey.

The story of Ingo Swann is fascinating. Did he really uncover evidence of a secret base on the Moon, one built and manned not by space-faring extraterrestrials but by good old humans? And why was Mr. Axelrod so intent in getting to the heart of the puzzle? Was he, perhaps, aware that some sort of secret space program existed and—for reasons unknown—looking to get to the bottom of the mystery? Perhaps he had been left *outside* of the loop, while dearly wishing to be *inside* it. Attempts have been made, on at least seven occasions, to use the Freedom of Information Act to (a) determine the true identity of Mr. Axelrod, (b) understand the nature of his agenda, (c) reveal the identity of the underground facility to which Swann was taken, and (d) identify all files and documents that might have been generated as a result of the Swann-Axelrod episode. Every attempt has completely failed. Nevertheless, the National Security Agency does admit to having a file on Ingo Swann—who passed away in January 2013—but refuses to release it. No matter the nature of the subject, it's always the same old story.

IN SEARCH OF AN ANTI-GRAVITY SPACE PLANE

From the early to mid-1990s, a young Welshman named Matthew Bevan—who happened to be a computer genius and definitive whiz-kid—decided it would be a fun and exciting thing to go digging into the most classified, computerized files of the U.S. military. Such actions are not fun and exciting. They are stupid and reckless, and are likely to cause you to deservedly end up in a small, well-guarded, concrete cell with nothing but walls for friends. Bevan chose to start with Wright-Patterson Air Force Base, which is located in Dayton, Ohio, and stressed that penetrating the computers of Wright-Patterson was, surprisingly, beyond easy. Bevan was near-dumbfounded to find that on barely his second or third penetration he stumbled upon a stash of classified files and e-mails dealing with a highly futuristic aircraft that had the ability to fly not just within the Earth's atmosphere, but *outside* of it, too. Bevan notes:

> On the one particular system that I got into, there was this flow of e-mail back and forth in which there was a discussion about some sort of radical engine that was being developed. People were discussing it in a normal work-type environment. They were talking about this engine and I recall one guy mentioned: 'We have managed to sustain mach-15 [Author's note: roughly 11,500 mph] and this thing is super-fast.' This was part of a discussion that was taking place between people at Wright-Patterson and there were explicit drawings, diagrams and so on, too. The files very clearly referred to a working prototype of an anti-gravity vehicle that utilized a heavy element to power it. This wasn't a normal aircraft; it was very small, split level, with a reactor at the bottom and room for the crew at the top (Redfern, 1998).

Bevan assumed that his illegal penetration of Wright-Patterson had gone unnoticed. He was dead wrong. On a weekday morning in early 1996, Bevan was arrested at his place of work (an insurance company in Cardiff, Wales) by Detective Sergeant Simon Janes of Scotland Yard's Computer Crimes Unit. The charge was serious: the hacking of Wright-Patterson, NASA, and a huge number of additional American military, intelligence, and governmental bodies. Bevan was now in big trouble. Interestingly, during the course of the initial interview with Bevan, the police kept coming back to that stash of files he read concerning some form of highly advanced aircraft that also, apparently, had the ability to break free of Earth's orbit and fly into space.

Bevan recalls of this particular line of questioning: "Throughout the interview, they kept coming back to: did I see anything on the Wright-Patterson and the NASA computers? Did I download anything? Well, when they asked me if I saw anything, I said: 'Yes, I saw e-mails talking about an anti-gravity propulsion system. But I didn't download them; I read them all online'" (Redfern, 1998).

The police were not impressed and Bevan was formally charged with hacking—a very serious charge that resulted in a 1997 trial at London's Bow Street magistrate's court. Surprisingly, the case against Bevan quickly crumbled like the walls of Jericho itself. The cause of the collapse was straightforward. The judge overseeing the case demanded to see evidence of Bevan's actions, and also evidence of the material he allegedly viewed online, regarding the military's secret space plane. U.S. authorities refused to show the judge any of the documentation. In fact, they refused to show anything. Unimpressed by this, the judge said that with the Americans refusing to agree to his request, there was no way Bevan could face time in jail. And any monetary fine would be meager. With prosecution costs running at around $10,000 a day, the U.S. government decided to drop its attempts to have Bevan nailed to the wall. The outcome was that Bevan walked free. His final word: "Although I didn't print or download anything, I know what I read: America has a secret space plane." To date, those files that Bevan accessed at Wright-Patterson—which even the judge overseeing the case back in 1997 wasn't allowed to view—have not surfaced into the public domain (Redfern, 1998).

SPACECRAFT OVER ENGLAND

Perhaps one of those fantastic aerial vehicles described in the files seen by Matthew Bevan was secretly flown over the UK, in the dead of night, on March 31, 1993. Numerous reports of an unidentified, triangular-shaped craft were made on the night in question—many of which were investigated by a British Ministry of Defense man, Nick Pope. Now retired from the MoD, Pope reveals his role in—and his knowledge of—the events in question:

The two most significant reports began at RAF Cosford [Author's note: a military base located in the English county of Shropshire]. This was definitely the highlight and was one of the best sighting reports I received in my entire posting. The report itself came from a guard patrol at Cosford. They were on duty manning entrance points, checking the perimeter fence and such like. All the members of the patrol saw the UFO and, again, the description was pretty much the same as most of the others. In this case, though, the UFO was at medium to high altitude. They didn't make a standard report: what they did was to submit an actual 2–3 page report which went up their chain of command and then the report was forwarded on to me. In that report, they stated that the UFO passed directly over the base and that this was of particular concern to them. They made immediate checks with various Air Traffic Control radar centers but nothing appeared on the screens. It was this factor that made them particularly keen to make an official report. This was at around 1:00 a.m. (Redfern, 1998).

Whatever the origin of the unknown vehicle, it appeared that its activities were far from over, as Pope notes graphically:

They noticed that this flying triangle was heading on a direct line for RAF Shawbury, which is some 12 to 15 miles on. Now, the main concern of the Cosford patrol was to alert Shawbury that the UFO was coming their way; but they also wanted confirmation that they weren't having a mass hallucination. They took a decision to call Shawbury and this was answered by the meteorological officer. You have to realize that at that time there was literally just a skeleton-staff operating, so the meteorological officer was, essentially, on his own. So, he took a decision to go outside, look in the direction of RAF Cosford and see what he could see. Sure enough, he could see this light coming towards him and it got closer and closer and lower and lower. Next thing, he was looking at this massive, triangular-shaped craft flying at what was a height of no more than two hundred feet, just to the side of the base and only about two hundred feet from the perimeter fence (Ibid.).

Bearing in mind the fact that the meteorological Officer at RAF Shawbury would have been considered a reliable witness and someone well-trained in recognizing numerous types of aerial phenomena, was he able to gauge the size of the object? Pope's response:

Very much so. Military officers are very good at gauging sizes of aircraft and they're very precise. His quote to me was that the UFO's size was

*midway between that of a C-130 Hercules and a Boeing 747 Jumbo Jet.
Now, he had eight years worth of experience with the Royal Air Force,
and a Met. Officer is generally much better qualified than most for looking at things in the night sky. And there were other factors too: he heard
this most unpleasant low-frequency hum, and he saw the craft fire a
beam of light down to the ground. He felt that it was something like a
laser beam or a searchlight. The light was tracking very rapidly back and
forth and sweeping one of the fields adjacent to the base (Ibid.).*

*He also said—and he admitted that this was speculation—that it was as
if the UFO was looking for something. Now, the speed of the UFO was
extremely slow—no more than twenty or thirty miles per hour, which in
itself is quite extraordinary. As far as the description is concerned, he said
that it was fairly featureless—a sort of flat, triangular-shaped craft, or
possibly a bit more diamond-shaped. But if all the descriptions had been
identical I would have been surprised (Ibid.).*

Perhaps the most eye-opening and revealing aspect of the RAF Shawbury
encounter was the way in which the object made its near-gravity-defying exit,
as Nick Pope now explains:

*He said that the beam of light retracted into the craft, which then seemed
to gain a little bit of height. But then, in an absolute instant, the UFO
moved from a speed of about twenty or thirty miles per hour to a speed
of several hundreds of miles per hour—if not thousands. It just suddenly
moved off to the horizon and then out of sight in no more than a second
or so—and there was no sonic boom. Well, of course, when I received this
report and the one from Cosford, I launched as full an investigation as I
possibly could (Ibid.).*

Many might suggest that this particular event had far more to do with matters of a UFO nature than secret military aircraft having the ability to fly into
deep space, as well as inside the Earth's atmosphere. It's most interesting, however, that the British Ministry of Defense made quiet approaches to the U.S.
government to see if they might have been the culprits. Obviously, someone
within the British Ministry of Defense had suspicions that this UFO may have
had origins of a domestic rather than extraterrestrial nature. Pope acknowl-
edges this:

*We decided that we couldn't ignore the various rumors that were do-
ing the rounds about a supposed top secret aircraft developed by the
U.S. Government and called Aurora—or, indeed, any hypersonic and/*

or prototype aircraft operated by the Americans. There had been persistent rumors in the aviation world and amongst the UFO lobby that the SR71 Blackbird had been replaced by a hypersonic aircraft code-named Aurora and that that was what the flying triangles really were. I was well aware that there had been some interesting stories about visual and radar sightings around certain air bases; however, I hadn't put much store in these rumors—not least because there had been some very definitive denials from the Americans (Ibid.).

Pope's office received an outright denial from the Americans that they were flying anything remotely like the rumored *Aurora*.

ANTI-GRAVITY FILES THAT CAN'T BE READ

Regardless of whether or not the craft seen at RAF Cosford and Shawbury in March 1993 was something akin to that described in the Wright-Patterson Air Force Base files uncovered by Matthew Bevan, it's interesting that back in 1956, a British magazine, *Aero Digest*, was tipped off to the fact that U.S. officials were secretly looking to harness the secrets of gravity for military and outer space gain. For two months, *Aero Digest* doggedly and intensively researched the tantalizing tidbits that came its way and ultimately published an article titled "Anti-Gravity Booming" in its March 1956 edition. A.V. Cleaver, commenting on the *Aero Digest* revelations in the *Journal of the British Interplanetary Society*, offered a notable statement: "The Americans have decided to look into the old science-fictional dream of gravity control, or 'anti-gravity,' to investigate, both theoretically and (if possible) practically the fundamental nature of gravitational fields and their relationship to electromagnetic and other phenomena." Remarkably, even back in the 1950s, the research was being carried out at Matthew Bevan's target of choice: Wright-Patterson Air Force Base. More than half a century after *Aero Digest* spilled the beans, the relevant documentation has still not been declassified (Cleaver, 1957).

Moving on, but still on the same topic, Marine Corps Major Donald E. Keyhoe noted in 1973 that research into gravity control seemed to fall under the auspices of the military and, more importantly, the domain of official secrecy. Commenting, in 1974, on the U.S. Air Force's early work in the field of gravity-control and gravity-manipulation, Keyhoe said: "When AF [Air Force] researchers fully realized the astounding possibilities, headquarters persuaded scientists, aerospace companies, and technical laboratories to set up anti-gravity projects, many of them under secret contracts. Every year, the number of projects increased" (Keyhoe, 1974).

Indeed, as far back as 1965, Keyhoe revealed, he had knowledge of no less than 46 programs linked to gravity-based research, of which more than 30 fell under the jurisdiction of the Air Force. I probably don't need to mention that the huge numbers of files that these collective projects must have generated have not seen the light of day.

THE STRANGE SAGA OF THE NON-TERRESTRIAL OFFICERS

Gary McKinnon, an Englishman and, like Matthew Bevan, an admitted computer hacker, lived for more than 10 years under the threat of extradition to the United States on charges of carrying out what one American prosecutor maintained was the largest computer hack of the U.S. official infrastructure in its history. McKinnon was also accused of causing severe damage to a whole host of NASA, defense, intelligence, and military-operated computer systems in the United States. When, in February 2001, McKinnon first elected to do something extremely stupid and assuredly not recommended—hack into the computer systems of the U.S. government for secret data—he did so from within the house of his girlfriend's aunt, in Crouch End, London. Jon Ronson, a writer who took an interest in McKinnon's situation, said: "Basically, what Gary was looking for—and found time and again—were network administrators within high levels of the U.S. government and military establishments who hadn't bothered to give themselves passwords. That's how he got in" (Ronson, 2005).

Having finally forced open the online door to NASA's secret stash of cosmic data, McKinnon found himself confronted by some truly weird material, including files that referenced what were intriguingly referred to as "Non Terrestrial Officers." The files, said McKinnon, contained lists of U.S. military personnel, their ranks, and evidence that they were engaged in certain, secret "off world" activities. McKinnon stressed: "It doesn't mean little green men. What I think it means is not Earth-based. I found a list of fleet-to-fleet transfers, and a list of ship names. I looked them up. They weren't U.S. navy ships." So whose ships, exactly, were they? McKinnon's conclusion: "What I saw made me believe they [Author's note: the U.S. military] have some kind of spaceship, off-planet" ("Hacker Feels US Navy Has Spaceships, Crews in Space," 2005).

Just like the Matthew Bevan affair, the case against Gary McKinnon collapsed. In October 2012, the British government's home secretary, Theresa

May, refused to hand over McKinnon to the Americans, who wanted him to stand trial in the United States. As for those files on the Non Terrestrial Officers, just like with the papers on that advanced anti-gravity space plane that Matthew Bevan found back in the 1990s, they're nowhere to be seen today.

THE U.S. SENATE TAKES NOTE

Then there were the eye-opening but cagey words of U.S. senators Jay Rockefeller and Ron Wyden who, in December 2004, spoke out on their awareness of secret, U.S. space-based activities during a fairly inflammatory exchange on the matter of the 2005 Intelligence Authorization Bill. It was a classified project that Rockefeller detailed as being incredibly expensive. He also revealed that, despite at least several attempts by the Senate to have the program closed down for good, all attempts to do so were quickly and authoritatively swept aside. Suggestions were made by Steven Aftergood of the Federation of American Scientists that the senators were talking, in careful and concise terms, about a top secret spy-satellite operation. This might well have been so.

In the bigger scheme of things, however, this affair—when combined with those of Matthew Bevan, Gary McKinnon, Karl Wolfe, Ingo Swann, Lieutenant General Arthur G. Trudeau, and Major Donald Keyhoe—demonstrates something very important: The domain of outer space is inextricably linked to military secrecy, advanced aviation-based technologies, and extremely well-hidden, classified programs that no one on the inside wants to talk about—and, certainly, no one wants to release any files on.

Now we come to our final section, which focuses on people who hold, or at least did hold, positions of power and prominence. Presidents, politicians, and powerful people who led us into war: They're all there.

PART 5: PRESIDENTS, POLITICIANS, AND POWERFUL PEOPLE

15: DEATH IN DALLAS

At 12:30 p.m., central time, on November 22, 1963, a nation-changing event occurred at Dealey Plaza in Dallas, Texas. It shocked not just the entire United States, but the world, too. In terms of that shock, and the subsequent, attendant outrage that developed in the days immediately afterwards, it's fair to say that it remained unparalleled until the equally tragic events of September 11, 2001. I am, of course, talking about the assassination of President John F. Kennedy. As the presidential motorcade traveled slowly along Dealey Plaza, and as huge throngs of onlookers waved, cheered, and took photos, shots rang out loudly, in rapid-fire procession. Chaos immediately broke out. People dived for cover. Confusion reigned. Amid all this, the life of the president came to a sudden, violent, and bloody end. Jacqueline Kennedy was left a widow, and Texas governor John Connally was seriously injured.

Less than two hours later Lee Harvey Oswald was in custody, having been found hiding out in the darkness of the Texas Theater, which is still open today and located in the Oak Cliff area of Dallas. Oswald was suspected of being behind the killing of both JFK and a local policeman, J.D. Tippit, who was shot shortly after the assassination, in Oak Cliff, as it transpires. Oswald was destined to never stand trial. On November 24th, he was also killed by a bullet. The man who ended the life of the man who maybe—or maybe not—shot the president was Jack Ruby, who owned Dallas' legendary Carousel Club. Ruby was found guilty of the murder of Oswald. But there was no life sentence for Ruby because he wasn't long for this earth, either. Ruby died on January 3, 1967, as a result of complications from lung cancer. Amid all of this death, there was an investigation into the assassination of President Kennedy that still provokes huge controversy to this day.

A study of the facts, testimony, and evidence that lasted for 10 months was undertaken by the President's Commission on the Assassination of President Kennedy. Or as it is better, albeit unofficially, known, the Warren Commission, which took its name from its chairman, Chief Justice Earl Warren. The commission was created on November 29, 1963 by the new president, Lyndon B. Johnson, who had been Kennedy's vice president. Its job was to get to the bottom of the big question that everyone wanted answered: Who killed JFK? According to the Warren Commission, it was Oswald. And it was only Oswald. Not everyone agreed with that controversial conclusion, however.

In 1978, 14 years after the commission laid all of the blame firmly on the shoulders of Oswald, the United States House Select Committee on Assassinations (HSCA) came to a startling, and very different, conclusion: President Kennedy's death was the result of a conspiracy. There are a number of misconceptions about the nature of the HSCA's findings. Many of those who have not read the committee's report have assumed that the HSCA considered Oswald to have been the definitive patsy that he loudly claimed to have been. Not so. The HSCA actually fully agreed with the Warren Commission that Kennedy was killed by Oswald and by no one else. The HSCA, however, went one step further, by concluding that Oswald was not the only gunman. Forensic analysis suggested to the HSCA's investigators that four shots rang out, not the three that the Warren Commission attributed to Oswald, on that day in Dealey Plaza. That's to say there was a second gunman. But, in the minds of the HSCA, this mysterious second shooter completely missed his target. Nevertheless, for the HSCA this left only one conclusion available to them. There was a distinct, high probability that two gunmen fired shots at Kennedy. Oswald hit his target—devastatingly so—but the elusive second gunman did not. But it still amounted to one thing: A conspiracy was at the heart of the JFK assassination.

Such is the never-ending interest in this admittedly tangled web of intrigue, it has spawned a veritable and definitive subculture, which has worked hard to try to uncover all of the available facts, data, and evidence on the presidential assassination. As a result of these actions, thousands upon thousands of previously classified documents on the murder of JFK—as well as additional files on numerous figures linked to the central players—have surfaced officially into the public domain. For all of those files that *have* surfaced, there's still a sizeable amount that *have not*. But you knew that was coming, right?

PRESIDENT'S COMMISSION
ON THE
ASSASSINATION OF PRESIDENT KENNEDY
200 Maryland Ave. N.E.
Washington, D.C.   20002
Telephone 543-1400

J. LEE RANKIN,
General Counsel

September 24, 1964

The President
The White House
Washington, D. C.

Dear Mr. President:

Your Commission to investigate the assassination
of President Kennedy on November 22, 1963, having completed
its assignment in accordance with Executive Order No. 11130
of November 29, 1963, herewith submits its final report.

Respectfully,

Earl Warren, Chairman

Richard B. Russell

John Sherman Cooper

Hale Boggs

Gerald R. Ford

Allen W. Dulles

John J. McCloy

A number of official documents on the JFK assassination of 1963 are suspiciously missing.
©U.S. Government Printing Office 1964

THE JFK FILES: CLOSED, DESTROYED, AND AVAILABLE

"It is a common misconception that the records relating to the assassination of President Kennedy are in some way sealed. In fact, the records are largely open and available to the research community here at the National Archives at College Park in the President John F. Kennedy Assassination Record Collection," states staff at the National Archives. Yes, most of the files that have been identified as having some relevance to the assassination are now in the public domain; there is little doubt about that. Because, however, the number of files and records that exist is so voluminous, even the small percentage that remains classified still amounts to a wealth of material. Before we get to the matter of what was sealed and what remains denied to us, though, let's see what is missing ("Frequently Asked Questions," 2013).

Those that loudly proclaim that the death of President Kennedy did not result from any sort of conspiracy often cite the fact that the U.S. government has now released the bulk of the available files on the affair into the public domain. If there was a conspiracy, so the argument goes, then why would officialdom make the records available? It sounds like a reasonable question. There is, however, one thing that often gets overlooked when it comes to this particular matter: We can prove that classified documentation relative to the assassination was destroyed long before the process of declassification ever began.

In other words, just because reams of material on the Kennedy assassination are in the public domain today, does not mean that just as many reams weren't shredded decades ago. And, perhaps, that material was shredded precisely because it *did* point in the direction of the domain of conspiracy. A classic and controversy-filled example is the strange saga of the destruction of the U.S. Army Intelligence file on Lee Harvey Oswald.

When, in the 1970s, the House Select Committee on Assassinations was busily trying to determine who shot and killed JFK, one of the people they interviewed was a retired U.S. Army colonel, Robert E. Jones. In an April 1978 interview with HSCA staff, Colonel Jones was, as the committee noted, the "commanding officer of the military intelligence region that encompassed Texas." Indeed, Jones,' official position was that of operations officer of the U.S. Army's 112th Military Intelligence Group at Fort Sam Houston, San Antonio, Texas (*Report of the Select Committee on Assassinations of the U.S. House of Representatives*, 1979).

Jones informed the HSCA that he knew for sure that somewhere between eight and 12 military intelligence operatives were in Dallas on the day of the

The Dallas, Texas–based Book Depository, from where, the Warren Commission concluded, Lee Harvey Oswald shot and killed JFK. ©Nick Redfern

assassination, reportedly to provide "supplemental security" for JFK's visit. Intrigued by this, the HSCA—already fast on its way to coming to a conclusion that there was a conspiracy behind the death of the president—did its utmost to identify the agents and examine all relevant files. Staff failed on both counts. The personnel in question could not be found, and the Department of Defense advised the HSCA that no records existed suggesting any kind of "Department of Defense Protective Services in Dallas." The HSCA summed up the situation with a few, choice words that speak volumes: "The committee was unable to resolve the contradiction" (Ibid.).

OSWALD'S MISSING INTELLIGENCE PAPERS

This was not the only example that the HSCA found where files that should have existed in relation to the Kennedy assassination did not. Certainly, the most intriguing example of the many that the HSCA uncovered revolved around Lee Harvey Oswald's Army Intelligence file. On the same day that Kennedy was killed in Dallas, Colonel Robert E. Jones contacted the FBI to report that he had information to share with them on Oswald, as well as the latter's alias of A.J. Hidell. The committee noted, correctly, as it would transpire: "This information suggested the existence of a military intelligence file on Oswald and raised the possibility that he [Oswald] had intelligence associations of some kind" (Ibid.).

HSCA records, which are now available to the public, show that its investigators were able to determine that Jones, in his official capacity as an Army intelligence operative, knew of Oswald and his activities as far back as June of 1963. The HSCA noted that this came via data that had been given to the 112th MIG (Military Intelligence Group) by sources within the New Orleans Police Department, "to the effect that Oswald had been arrested there in connection with Fair Play for Cuba Committee activities." Having acquired this data, HSCA records show, the 112th Military Intelligence Group "took an interest in Oswald as a possible counterintelligence threat" (Ibid.).

The 112th MIG did more than just take an interest in Oswald; it opened a secret file on the man. The file reportedly contained photocopies of newspaper articles and documents related to Oswald's decision to defect to the Soviet Union in October 1959, his activities and associations in Russia, his subsequent return to the United States, and his "pro-Cuba" activities in New Orleans and other parts of Louisiana (Ibid.).

When Colonel Jones heard the news about Oswald being taken into custody shortly after the assassination, he quickly contacted the FBI in Dallas to inform them that Army Intelligence had a file on Oswald and advised its agents of the file's contents. Jones testified to the HSCA that his next—and, as it happened, final—act on this matter was to prepare an "after action" summary-style report that described "the actions he had taken, the people he had notified and the times of notification." That summary also contained data relative to those military intelligence personnel who, in plain clothes, were in Dealey Plaza when Kennedy was shot dead. Jones stated that, to his complete amazement, there was nothing but overwhelming silence after he approached the FBI. The Bureau staff, the Secret Service, the Warren Commission, and the CIA all had one thing in common: They carefully avoided speaking with Jones on the matter of the assassination in general, and on Oswald and his Army intelligence file in particular (Ibid.).

With Jones's information in hand, the HSCA set about getting hold of the intelligence file on Oswald. Not a chance of that happening, as the committee noted: "Access to Oswald's military intelligence file, which the Department of Defense never gave to the Warren Commission, was not possible because the Department of Defense had destroyed the file as part of a general program aimed at eliminating all of its files pertaining to nonmilitary personnel" (Ibid.).

Suspecting that there was far more than just mere bureaucracy at the heart of the destruction of the Oswald records, the HSCA demanded that the Department of Defense provide it with a full explanation of the circumstances that led to the irreversible loss of the Oswald file. The DoD replied that although the file was noted for shredding on March 1, 1973, it was "not possible" to ascertain, precisely, the date on which the "physical destruction was accomplished." The DoD assured the HSCA that the destruction had been a purely routine matter, and not in any way suspicious. There was, however, a hell of a lot that could not be ascertained: "It is not possible to determine who accomplished the actual physical destruction of the dossier," said the DoD, adding: "The individual ordering the destruction or deletion cannot be determined." And, perhaps, most significant of all, on the matter of the actual contents of the file, the DoD told the HSCA: "The exact material contained in the dossier cannot be determined." The DoD did, however, suggest that the file "most probably" included "several Federal Bureau of Investigation reports, and possibly some Army counterintelligence reports" (Ibid.).

Far from satisfied by this reply, the HSCA requested that the Department of Defense provide them with a copy of the actual destruction order concerning the intelligence dossier on Oswald. The reply was swift but, yet again, far from satisfactory, as far as the HSCA was concerned: "Army regulations do not require any type of specific order before intelligence files can be destroyed, and none was prepared in connection with the destruction of the Oswald file" (Ibid.).

In light of the above, it's worth noting the HSCA's conclusions on this particular matter: "The committee found this 'routine' destruction of the Oswald file extremely troublesome, especially when viewed in light of the Department of Defense's failure to make this file available to the Warren Commission. Despite the credibility of Jones' testimony, without access to this file, the question of Oswald's possible affiliation with military intelligence could not be fully resolved" (Ibid.).

This saga is important for two reasons: (a) it demonstrates that regardless of what the government, today, places into the public domain on the assassination, important data that could have shed a great deal of light on the death of JFK was destroyed decades ago; and (b) it was one of more than a few such examples of missing papers—and possibly suspiciously missing papers—that the HSCA uncovered during the course of its investigation into the president's death.

THE PROCESS OF DECLASSIFICATION

When the Warren Commission wrapped up its work in 1964, the files that had been created as a result of its investigation were transferred to the National

Archives for safe keeping. The papers that were not made public—or publicized—in the Warren Commission's report were subject to an executive order that effectively sealed them until 2039. The reason: "to serve as protection for innocent persons who could otherwise be damaged because of their relationship with participants in the case." Quite understandably, the process of denying pretty much anyone and everyone access to the records until all those who might have had some knowledge of the matter would be long dead, only served to inflame the claims that a conspiracy lay at the heart of the killing of JFK. Those claims of conspiracy were elevated to stratospheric levels in the immediate aftermath of the release of Oliver Stone's 1991 movie on the assassination, *JFK*, which starred Kevin Costner as New Orleans District Attorney Jim Garrison and Gary Oldman as Lee Harvey Oswald (*Report of the President's Commission on the Assassination of President Kennedy*, 1964).

As a result of the huge publicity given to the movie, and the reignited, nationwide interest in the conspiracy theories surrounding Kennedy's killing, the U.S. Congress passed what was named the Kennedy Assassination Records Collection Act of 1992. The act led to the creation of the Assassination Records Review Board (ARRB). Part of its work was to make recommendations and decisions when an agency of the U.S. government office refused to make available its records on the JFK assassination. There was solid justification for this. The act required every federal agency of government to turn over to the National Archives all records relating to the assassination. Today, that collection of open data on the events of November 22, 1963, runs to more than five million pages, from such sources as the Warren Commission, the John F. Kennedy, Lyndon B. Johnson, and Gerald Ford Presidential Libraries, the CIA, the FBI, and the Office of Naval Intelligence.

"With a very few exceptions," says the National Archives, "virtually all of the records identified as belonging to the Kennedy Collection have been opened in part or in full." It should be noted, however, that "virtually all" is not all ("Frequently Asked Questions," 2013).

ONE PERCENT OF FIVE MILLION PAGES

In the summer of 2012, the matter of how much material on the JFK assassination the government was still withholding, from the public and media alike, became a big talking point. On June 12th, a press release was circulated by a Washington, D.C. non-profit public interest group called the Assassination Archives and Research Center (AARC). At the heart of the press release were the AARC's comments concerning a National Archives' assistant archivist named Michael Kurtz. As the AARC noted, in 2010, at a public forum, Kurtz had stated that the remaining closed material on the Kennedy assassination would be available by the end of 2013.

The AARC noted in its press release, however: "The Archives today says that Kurtz 'misspoke' when he made that commitment to the public. Kurtz's promise to process the secret JFK related documents fulfilled President Obama's expressed desire that his administration be the most open in history. Today's reversal of release of these records defeats President Obama's pledge that his be the most open administration in history." Also noted by the AARC was the fact that the National Archives confirmed that no less than 1,171 "classified documents" on the JFK assassination were still being held by the CIA. How many pages this might all run to is a matter of debate ("National Archives Decides to Withhold Records Related to the Assassination of President John F. Kennedy," 2012).

The National Archives states that it "does not know the actual number of pages that are postponed in full." Dr. Kurtz, Archives staff note, "accurately stated that 'less than one percent' of the total volume of assassination records was still being withheld." Because Kurtz also provided a "rough estimate" of five million pages that were still outside of the public arena, one percent of five million pages would equate to around 50,000 pages. We can't be sure of the exact figure, because, as the National Archives admits: "All we do know is that the CIA withheld in full a total of 1,171 documents as national security classified" (Stern, 2012).

The National Archives also revealed that, as a result of the growing interest in the assassination—largely prompted by its 50th anniversary on November 22, 2013—its staff had been "consulting with the CIA." The purpose was to determine if it would be feasible for the latter to undertake its review of the 1,171 documents, and have them in the public domain in time for the anniversary. Good news was not forthcoming, as the National Archives demonstrated: "Although the CIA shares NARA's interest in wanting to be responsive to your request, they have concluded there are substantial logistical requirements that must take place prior to the release of these remaining records and there is simply not sufficient time or resources to complete these tasks prior to 2017" (Ibid.).

Will we see these remaining files in 2017? Time will tell. To what extent they will shed any further light on the true circumstances surrounding the assassination of President John F. Kennedy at Dealey Plaza, Dallas, Texas, on that early afternoon of November 22, 1963, remains to be seen—or, maybe, not to be seen. And on the subject of things not to be seen, it's now time to focus our attention on the secrets of one of the United States' most powerful figures of all time.

16: HOOVER'S SECRET FILES GET HOOVERED

J. Edgar Hoover, the near-legendary director of the Federal Bureau of Investigation, was born on January 1, 1895. Although the FBI, itself, was not created until 1935, it did have a predecessor. It was the similarly named Bureau of Investigation, of which Hoover was also director, from 1924 onward. With the establishment of the FBI, however, the United States finally had a nation-wide, domestic intelligence-gathering agency that fought crime—and usually won the battle, sometimes violently—on a daily basis.

Gangsters, such as George "Machine Gun Kelly" Barnes, Al Capone, John Dillinger, Charles Arthur "Pretty Boy" Floyd, and many others, were all the subjects of FBI investigations—and even shoot-outs—in its early years. During the Second World War, much of the FBI's work was focused on eliminating the serious threat posed by Nazi and Japanese agents operating within the United States. In the post-war era, concerns about Germany and Japan were gone. They were, however, replaced by an even more formidable, potential foe: the Soviet Union. Much attention was given during the early years of the Cold War to ferreting out Russian spies, undercover agents acting on behalf of their masters in the Kremlin, and U.S. citizens who had turned traitorous. It was during this period that Hoover's FBI massively increased its surveillance of the Mafia and the world of organized crime. The Bureau also spent a great deal of time secretly watching the activities of numerous famous faces, as we have already seen in relation to Marilyn Monroe, for example. In the 1960s, much manpower was spent secretly monitoring Martin Luther King, Jr., the Civil Rights movement, and activist Malcolm X. Today, of course, domestic terrorism is at the forefront of the FBI's important work. Tens of thousands of pages of formerly classified FBI documents—covering all of the above topics and many more—are now freely available at the FBI's Website, the Vault. One key collection, however, is missing.

THE "SECRET FILES"

J. Edgar Hoover was noted for his dedication to the compilation of files on just about anyone and everyone that he saw as being ripe and relevant for covert surveillance. But, as well as the regular files that the FBI created and updated on a daily basis—namely, the ones that are now online at the Vault—Hoover had at his disposal another collection of documentation—a very different and unique collection. It was one deemed for his eyes only. That collection was highly sensitive and filled with all sorts of gossip, scandal, national security data, and deep secrets on a lot of high-profile individuals. Indeed, Curt Gentry, a respected authority on the life and career of J. Edgar Hoover, notes of the secret files that they were focused on such matters as "blackmail material on the patriarch of an American political dynasty, his sons, their wives, and other women; allegations of two homosexual arrests which Hoover leaked to help defeat a witty, urbane Democratic presidential candidate; the surveillance reports on one of America's best-known first ladies and her alleged lovers, both male and female, white and black." And, not forgetting, "the forbidden fruit of hundreds of illegal wiretaps and bugs" (Gentry, 2001).

The voluminous document collection in question has become infamously known as the *Secret Files*. Unfortunately for historians, Hoover's classified records—and the full and unexpurgated tales they told—will never make it to the Vault. After Hoover's death, from heart disease, on May 2, 1972, those same files were quickly destroyed. The secrets those voluminous papers told went, just like Hoover, to the grave. Fortunately, however, the story of how and why those documents came to be destroyed certainly did not follow suit. It all revolves around an old lady, a septuagenarian, who was fiercely loyal to her boss, J. Edgar Hoover. Her name was Helen Gandy, and she outwitted everyone as she sought to ensure Hoover's secrets didn't become open knowledge.

BACKING UP THE BOSS

Born in 1897, two years after J. Edgar Hoover's birth, Helen Gandy was Hoover's personal secretary for more than half a century. And she was as faithful

J. Edgar Hoover, the legendary director of the FBI from 1935 to 1972. ©U.S. government

to her boss at the very end as she was at the very beginning. For Gandy, the work with Hoover began in 1918, when she started working, as a clerk, for the Justice Department. Less than a month later, she was doing work for Hoover, chiefly typing memoranda and documentation. Although the Hoover-Gandy relationship was purely a professional one, the pair had two things in common: (a) Neither had any meaningful interest in settling down, getting married, and having kids; and (b) both were unswervingly dedicated to the task of making, and maintaining, the FBI as the world's leading and most respected crime fighting organization. As a sign of the respect that Hoover had for Gandy, her job description as a typist was upgraded, in 1937, to office assistant. Two years later, she was given the title of executive assistant. She certainly proved to be indispensable to Hoover in the immediate aftermath of his death on May 2, 1972.

There is a degree of controversy surrounding Hoover's passing. Although there is no hard evidence to suggest Hoover's death was in any fashion suspicious—he was, after all, 77 years of age and suffering from cardiovascular disease at the time—there are questions about who found Hoover's body on the floor of his bedroom. Some researchers suggest that it was Hoover's personal cook, Annie Fields. Others maintain it was James Crawford, who had been Hoover's driver for nearly 40 years, and who was then recently retired. Either way, we know what happened next. Fields quickly telephoned Hoover's personal doctor, Dr. Robert V. Choisser, and broke the bad news to him. Choisser headed for Hoover's residence and examined the body at about 9 a.m. It would not be long before word got out that an American legend had died at some point after 10:00 p.m. on the night before. Oddly enough, and something that admittedly does fan the flames of conspiracy to a degree, Hoover's body was never autopsied. Whether or not this is of any significance to anything is debatable. But, in the minds of some, there was a far more pressing matter than that of an autopsy; there were those secret files to be dealt with. And they had to be dealt with swiftly.

THE COUNTDOWN TO DESTRUCTION

After having examined Hoover's body, and confirmed his death, Dr. Robert V. Choisser then telephoned a man named Clyde Tolson, who held the position of associate director of the FBI from 1930 to 1972. Because both Hoover and Tolson were bachelors, regularly had dinner together, and even holidayed together, this has given rise to rumors, of varying degrees of credibility, that their relationship was a sexual one. Nothing, though, has ever gone further than rumor and innuendo. Tolson, shocked to the core by the news, called Helen Gandy. In no uncertain terms, Tolson made it clear that it was time to clear out Hoover's secret stash, which filled a number of large filing cabinets at FBI headquarters. There is, however, some evidence to suggest that Gandy, knowing of Hoover's health issues, may actually have started the process of destruction before Hoover's passing, but on his specific orders. In early 1975, the *New York Times* reported on the words of an FBI agent who preferred to speak strictly off the record about Hoover's Secret Files. On the matter of their destruction, the agent told the newspaper that Gandy actually began shredding the files nearly a year before Hoover passed away.

One day after Hoover's death there was a new boss in town. His name was Louis Patrick Gray III, who took on the position of acting director of the FBI until April 1973. Gray resigned from the FBI, in disgrace, that month when it was determined that he had illegally shredded documents to protect the Nixon administration during the Watergate scandal, which just happens to be the subject of the next chapter. Ironically, the bulk of the work that usually fell under Hoover's jurisdiction was, after his death, undertaken by the FBI's associate director, Mark Felt. I say "ironically" because Felt was none other than the infamous "Deep Throat," whose revelations to journalists Bob Woodward and Carl Bernstein finally toppled, and equally disgraced, President Richard Nixon.

DEFLECTING THE NEW ACTING DIRECTOR

When Louis Patrick Gray III became acting director of the Bureau, his first task—which is rumored to have come directly, loudly, and in lightning-speed time, from President Nixon himself—was to secure Hoover's secret files, no matter what the consequences were. Helen Gandy, shrewdly anticipating that something like this might happen, was way ahead of both Nixon and Gray. When Gray got to Hoover's office, Gandy skillfully sidelined him and offered to give him a tour of FBI headquarters. Perhaps feeling that, as the new acting director, he should at least have some understanding of the place where he would be working, Gray politely, but maybe grudgingly, agreed to take the tour. Behind the scenes, this was giving Gandy's trusted colleagues more time to dig out all of the sensitive files that had been flagged for shredding.

Despite Gandy's plan to try to ensure that Gray didn't see any evidence of the large-scale removal of Hoover's papers that was going on, it was perhaps inevitable, amid all of the chaos, that Gray would get wind of something. And he did. In several rooms, Gray couldn't fail to notice that there were a number of conspicuously empty filing cabinets. When Gray—attempting to conceal that he was there to try to take charge of Hoover's files for Nixon—inquired about the empty cabinets, Gandy brushed him off. She asserted that the records that had been stored there were Hoover's personal papers, and they had merely been boxed up for transfer to Hoover's home. Gandy assured Gray that these were tax records and medical files—nothing of a secret nature. She also assured him that the many FBI personnel who were busily loading additional files into boxes were also simply collecting together Hoover's personal materials, none of which, she added for good measure, was directly related to the work of the FBI. Additionally, Gandy explained that it would take about a week to get Hoover's office empty and ready for Gray, so he would have to find another office to work from in the meantime. Gandy was playing a masterly game of chess with a man whom she clearly outwitted and ultimately checkmated.

Gray, however, thought he was the one with the upper hand. He told Nixon that he had taken steps to ensure that Hoover's office and all of its contents remained as they were when he, Gray, arrived on site. Gray announced to the press, smugly and overly self-assured, that he had taken firm steps to ensure the integrity of the files remained intact. He failed to realize, though, that not only did Hoover have a private office—his personal, inner sanctum—but he also had a veritable suite of *additional* offices. Chiefly, these extra rooms were created to cope with the voluminous flow of documentation that the FBI generated daily.

J. Edgar Hoover (right) with Clyde Tolson, the FBI's associate director. ©L.A. Times, *1939*

One of these areas was termed the Outer Office, which was the well-protected territory of Helen Gandy, and where much of Hoover's classified material was stored. It seemingly never occurred to Gray that Gandy's office area, rather than Hoover's, was home to the Aladdin's Cave of secrets that he so desperately sought to acquire for the president.

Two days after Hoover's death, Gandy met with Mark Felt and presented him with a dozen large boxes. Collectively, they were comprised of more than 150 case files, and close to 20,000 pages of material—all of it highly classified and much of it said to have been controversial in nature. A great deal of shredding was soon underway. This, however, was just the appetizer. Hoover's private records (the secret files) were still yet to come. For no less than 10 days, Gandy, who maintained control of those particular documents, diligently and devotedly scrutinized every one of Hoover's most guarded dossiers, despite Gray's failed efforts to take charge of the situation. She did so in her own office, practically right under the nose of the new acting director!

On top of that, in excess of 30 large file drawers of documentation were driven to Hoover's home by agents specifically loyal to their now-deceased director and placed for safe keeping in the basement. Over the following four days, reviewing and shredding continued at a steady pace, while John P. Mohr, the Assistant to the director for administrative affairs, kept a careful and close watch on every step of the process. Even James Jesus Angleton—who headed the CIA's counterintelligence office from 1954 to 1975—was on hand to assist in the destruction. There are, however, stories that some of the material that Angleton handled didn't get destroyed but was, instead, liberated by the man himself. Finally, after days of Gandy and Co. toiling tirelessly in the basement, Hoover's secrets were safe from penetration. That's to say, they were destroyed—aside, that is, from whatever the nature of the documents that James Jesus Angleton managed to secure for his own, and unknown, covert reasons.

AWKWARD QUESTIONS AND AWKWARD ANSWERS

In 1975, three years after Hoover's files were purged and destroyed, Helen Gandy found herself in profoundly hot water. She was ordered to testify before the House Committee on Government Oversight. At the time, the committee was looking into the matter of J. Edgar Hoover's obsessive, and—in terms of privacy violation—possibly highly illegal, surveillance operations that targeted Martin Luther King, Jr., in the 1960s. Gandy admitted to the committee that records, beyond just those that the FBI admitted to having on file, did exist. For a while, they did. Gandy stated forthrightly to the committee that she shredded the papers and put all of the tattered remains into boxes. Just for good measure, added Gandy, the boxes were all taken to an FBI field office, where they were burned.

When the committee turned its attention to Hoover's secret files, Gandy stood by the assertion of 1972 that she had given to Acting Director Louis Patrick Gray III. Namely, that the only documents destroyed after Hoover's death were ones that were personal to Hoover himself. Personal letters and documentation concerning the pedigrees of Hoover's pet dogs were near the top of Gandy's innocuous list. Gandy's response was not surprisingly met with overwhelming skepticism by the committee, to which she replied, in assertive tones, that she had no reason to tell an untruth. Andrew Maguire, of the 94th Congress, said he found it all a bit too much to believe. Gandy hit back by saying that was his right. Game over.

When J. Edgar Hoover died, a piece of Helen Gandy went with him. Although she was at the helm of the operation that ensured Hoover's most classified records never saw the light of day, she chose to retire from the FBI on hearing the news that her boss for more than half a century was no more. Hoover left Gandy $5,000 in his will, an undeniable act of kindness for a man hardly noted for showing much in the way of deep emotion. Gandy lived in the Washington, D.C. area until 1986, when she moved to Florida. She died of a heart attack at the age of 91 on July 7, 1988. Her loyalty to J. Edgar Hoover was intact to the end, as was her version of events concerning what happened to that enormous stack of secret files.

We now have to take a look at yet another powerful figure in politics that also had on hand a highly devoted character that helped to protect her boss by destroying vital, incriminating data.

17: WIPING THE SLATE CLEAN

It was a saga filled to the brim with conspiracy, illegal activity, shadowy characters, and a multitude of strange twists and turns. And, in the end, it led to the shameful resignation of an American president. It was, if you have not yet deduced, Watergate. It all began shortly after midnight on June 17, 1972, when the headquarters of the Democratic National Committee played host to a number of uninvited visitors. Their names were Frank Sturgis, James McCord, Bernard Barker, Eugenio Martinez, and Virgilio Gonzalez. The headquarters itself was located in the Watergate Complex, a collection of apartments, offices, and a hotel, the construction of which was finished in 1971, and sited in the Foggy Bottom district of Washington, D.C. The five conspirators were there to install covert audio-surveillance equipment and make surreptitious photocopies of various important documents related to the work of the Democratic Party. The plan was to break in, secure the bugs where they wouldn't be found, copy the papers, and get out—all as soon as conceivably possible. Matters didn't go as planned and anticipated, however.

Thanks to the actions of Frank Wills—a security guard on duty that night—the team of McCord, Sturgis, Martinez, Gonzalez, and Barker was caught red-handed by police officers, right inside the office of the Democratic National Committee, no less. What, at first, seemed to be a break-in that implicated the five men and no one else, quickly mutated into something acutely different. A substantial amount of cash was found on the five. Its point of origin was found to be the Committee for the Reelection of the President, the body that coordinated the presidential campaign of then-President Richard Milhous Nixon. Not surprisingly, the Nixon administration did their best to deny any links between the actions of the five men at the Watergate Complex and the president himself. As history has infamously demonstrated, though, their best was simply not good enough. As the FBI, local police, and the nation's media began to dig deeper and deeper, shocking discovery upon shocking discovery was made.

The origins of the affair that brought the presidency of Richard Nixon to a crashing halt began in January 1972 with G. Gordon Liddy, a former FBI man who became the agency's youngest bureau supervisor. He attained the position while still in his 20s. But that was back in 1960, and the world was a very different place by 1972. Liddy came up with a plan to conduct what amounted to a series of illegal operations against the Democratic Party, and that were designed to help benefit the Nixon presidency. Liddy's ideas were shared with three powerful men: John Dean, Jeb Magruder, and John Mitchell. Dean held the significant position of White House Counsel, which basically meant he was the chief adviser to Nixon on all matters of a legal nature. Mitchell was the attorney general, and Magruder was the acting chairman of the Committee for the Reelection of the President. Though the ideas of Liddy were seen as somewhat over-ambitious, around eight weeks later, a tentative plan was given the unofficial go-ahead to target the office of the Democratic National Committee.

In the days, weeks, and months that followed the arrest of the five-man team on June 17, 1972, the claims that the Nixon administration was not tied to the matter, to some degree, became more untenable and unsupportable. Extensive inquiries made by journalists Bob Woodward and Carl Bernstein, of *All the President's Men* fame, uncovered an extensive body of people linked, in varying capacities, to the Watergate break-in and to the White House itself. Then there was the damning evidence that, regardless of the extent of the White House's knowledge of, and involvement in, the matter, Nixon himself had tried to cover up any presidential connections to the events of June 17th, chiefly as a form of damage control. As a result, what began as an investigation of a burglary became something that, on August 9, 1974, led to the toppling of President Nixon. On top of that monumental development, numerous individuals that held positions of great responsibility and power in the Nixon administration found themselves in jail. To say that the affair shook the entire nation is not an exaggeration.

It's highly ironic that the Watergate affair began with a plan to bug the office of the Democratic National Committee. The reason: Nixon was himself a big advocate of clandestinely recording as many of his own conversations and discussions as conceivably possible. Those recordings, which were disclosed during the course of the Watergate investigations, confirmed that Nixon had tried to cover up the White House connection to the crime. The president, in an odd and perhaps appropriately karma-driven fashion, had sealed his own fate. But, while studying the vast amount of White House tapes that Nixon had compiled during his presidency, it was learned that no less than 18 minutes of one particular tape had been mysteriously wiped clean. That cleansing, and who was responsible and why, still provokes debate and intrigue years down the line.

President Richard Nixon, who was forced to resign from office as a result of Watergate. ©U.S. government, 1973

NIXON: THE MAN WITH HIS FINGER ON THE BUTTON (THE ONE MARKED "RECORD")

Had it not been for Watergate, it's possible that the world would never have had any knowledge of President Nixon's predilection for recording, almost to the point of obsession, his own conversations with White House staff and government, military, and intelligence personnel. It was only when the Senate Watergate Committee—which was tasked with investigating the scandal—began addressing the matter of how much Nixon knew of the Watergate Complex penetration that the existence of the tapes became known.

It was not out of the question for presidents to occasionally record their White House–based conversations. Franklin D. Roosevelt, Dwight D. Eisenhower, John F. Kennedy, and Lyndon B. Johnson had all done exactly that. But there were big differences. Nixon's predecessors were open and up-front about their recordings, whereas the man for whom Watergate proved to be his downfall, assuredly was not open about such matters. When any of the previous four wished to have their conversations and debates preserved, recording equipment was brought into the Oval Office and turned on in the presence of those sitting in on the meeting, briefing, or whatever may have been on the day's agenda. Nixon's approach was very different. It was tantamount to downright snooping. With extreme stealth, in February 1971, Nixon ordered that surveillance equipment should be secretly installed, and hidden, in certain rooms of the White House. This included both microphones and wire taps. The specific rooms targeted were the Cabinet Room, the Lincoln Sitting Room, the Oval Office, and the Old Executive Office Building. An ambitious Nixon even decided to bug the presidential retreat at Camp David. All of the work was undertaken by the Secret Service, while the ever-growing body of recordings was stored in a secure part of the White House's basement.

It didn't matter if Nixon or his most trusted aides weren't around when someone they might want to get on tape was in the White House, because all of the equipment was designed to be voice-activated. Perhaps *1600* Pennsylvania Avenue Northwest should have been renamed *1984* Pennsylvania Northwest. For around two and a half years, the equipment did its thing, recording more than 3,500 hours of conversation onto literally hundreds of tapes. Only when the Senate Watergate Committee got word of what was outrageously afoot was the prying program finally shut down. July 18, 1973 marked the day when Nixon's secret bugs eavesdropped for their last time. Suspiciously, barely 200 of those 3,500 hours referred to Watergate. This has led many Watergate investigators in both government and the media to conclude that certain tapes had been deemed for nobody's eyes only. They could well have been 100 percent correct in that conclusion. It's time to examine the curious affair of Rose Mary Woods and certain recordings that were wiped into oblivion—accidentally, Woods wanted everyone to believe. Many, however, did not in the slightest.

A TERRIBLE MISTAKE VS. PROTECTING THE PRESIDENT

Unsurprisingly, when the press, the FBI, and the Senate Watergate Committee got word that Nixon liked to indulge in a great deal of audio-based voyeurism, the president flat-out refused to make the tapes and their contents public. He angrily argued that because matters related to the national security of the United States were discussed in many of the recordings kept on file, there

Advisory Panel
on White House Tapes
May 31, 1974

Judge John J. Sirica
United States District Court
for the District of Columbia
Washington, D.C.

Dear Judge Sirica:

We are pleased to submit herewith the final report on our
technical investigation of a tape recorded in the Executive
Office Building on June 20, 1972. This is the tape on which an
eighteen and one-half minute section of buzz appears.

The report itself occupies the first fifty pages of this volume.
The remaining pages contain appended material concerning our
study, followed by a set of detailed Technical Notes on the
scientific techniques we used and the test results we obtained.

Respectfully yours,

Richard H. Bolt
Richard H. Bolt

Franklin S. Cooper
Franklin S. Cooper

James L. Flanagan
James L. Flanagan

John G. McKnight
John G. McKnight

Thomas G. Stockham, Jr.
Thomas G. Stockham, Jr.

Mark R. Weiss
Mark R. Weiss

*In 1974, an official inquiry was launched into the matter of missing audio recordings from
the Nixon White House. ©Advisory Panel on White House Tapes, 1974*

was no way this material could be released without affecting the safety of the nation. The Senate Watergate Committee was having none of it, however, and demanded that the tapes be released for independent scrutiny. A concerned Nixon caved in—to a degree, anyway. He suggested, outrageously and amusingly, that the tapes should be handed over to a man named John C. Stennis for scrutiny. Stennis was a Democrat and a senator. He was also significantly deaf. The committee was not impressed by Nixon's strange humor and his suggestion that the audio recordings be reviewed by someone whose hearing was hardly up to par. Archibald Cox, who had served as the U.S. solicitor general under JFK, and who was the special prosecutor in the Watergate fiasco, essentially told the president to take a flying leap. In response, Nixon tried to get the then-attorney general, Elliot Richardson, to have Cox removed. To his credit, Richardson refused Nixon's orders and quickly resigned his position. Time was soon up for Nixon, too.

One thing in particular that was apparent when the Nixon tapes became public knowledge, and also became a staple part of the Watergate inquiry, was that a portion of one tape made on June 20, 1972, was missing. More correctly, someone had recorded over that portion, which amounted to 18 and a half minutes. It was all a big mistake, we are led to believe. Although there are more holes in the story than in a block of Swiss cheese, there's no denying who the culprit was: Rose Mary Woods, who served as Nixon's personal secretary. She was noted for her unswerving loyalty to Nixon, which dated back to when she first became his secretary in 1951. Perhaps that loyalty led her to become the fall guy—or the fall gal—in what remains a mystery decades later.

Woods's version of events went like this. It was September 29, 1973, and she was busy transcribing a recording made on June 20, 1972. As she listened to the recording, Woods made what she claimed to have been an error of gigantic proportions. If a mistake was all it really was, then it was indeed terrible. But, if not, then it was an outrageous attempt to hide something that still remains hidden—or, more correctly, lost—to this day. While Woods was hard at work transcribing, the telephone rang. Woods then, she said, did two things: She (a) reached to answer the call, and (b) pressed the "stop" button on the tape-player. Or, rather, she didn't. She *meant* to hit "stop," but actually hit a button labeled "record" instead. Unfathomably, she also kept her foot on a floor pedal that allowed for an earlier recording to be taped over. Only after the call ended did Woods realize that more than 18 minutes of priceless data was now forever gone. Oddly, the call lasted for barely five minutes. We know that because it was recorded onto the tape. Woods had no answer, however, for what had happened to the additional 13 minutes of material, which, a study of the tape showed, had been replaced by nothing but constant electronic buzzing.

STRETCHING CREDIBILITY TO THE FINEST POINT POSSIBLE

When brought before a grand jury on June 23 and 24, 1975, Richard Nixon claimed to have no recollection of the original conversation that was now gone for good. That it was recorded only three days after the Watergate break-in, though, convinced many observers that the conversation had to have been on that same topic. Certainly, none could deny the timing was right for such a conversation to have occurred. As for who Nixon might have been speaking with, most of the fingers were pointed in the direction of Harry Robbins Haldeman, Nixon's chief of staff, whose records show *did* speak with Nixon on that same day. Nixon, when forcibly pressed for answers, claimed not to have recalled any such conversation, never mind the actual nature of its content.

Faithful Rose continued to stand by her man, so to speak, when the grand jury demanded she show them how she managed to press "record," then answer the phone, while keeping her foot on the pedal, and all at the same time. Had the phone been on the desk in front of her, it would have been a relatively easy process to achieve. Except the phone wasn't in front of her, and the process certainly was not easy. The phone in question was actually *behind* Woods at the time. This required her to make a monumental stretch to ensure that the phone could be answered at the same time as the pedal was firmly depressed and the "record" button was pushed. That the same stretch had to be held for at least five minutes—and maybe as many as 18—by a then 55-year-old woman, only (pardon the pun) stretched credibility to even further levels of the unlikely kind. Such was the notoriety that Woods's elaborate and improbable show before the jury provoked, it became known wryly among the Washington, D.C. media as the "Rose Mary Stretch." It wasn't just the media that expressed doubts about Woods's version of events. Even former White House Chief of Staff Alexander Haig suggested that Nixon may have been the culprit all along and that Woods agreed to play the role of the guilty party. At the very least, said Haig, he felt there had been shadowy forces at work in the matter of the recordings.

It's worth noting, too, the conclusions of the Advisory Panel on White House Tapes that carefully studied the recording and prepared, on May 31, 1974, an 87-page report on the matter. In part, the authors of the report said that: "The buzz sound probably originated in electrical noise on the electrical power line that powered the recorder. Any speech sounds previously recorded on this section of the tape were erased in conjunction with the recording process, as is normal in recorders of this kind. The erasure is so strong as to make recovery of the original conversation virtually impossible" ("The EOB Tape of June 20, 1972," 2013).

The authors of the document also stated: "This report draws no inferences about such questions as whether the erasure and buzz were made accidentally or intentionally, or when, or by what person or persons. The report does provide a solid basis in experimental fact for concluding that the erasure and the recording of buzz required several operations of the pushbuttons on the control keyboard of the Uher 5000 recorder" (Ibid.).

This final reference to "several operations of the pushbuttons" is, of course, at odds with the claims of Rose Mary Woods, who said she hit just one button ("record") once and once only. I will leave it to you to decide whose version of events we should accept as being most likely: that of a woman who had been deeply loyal to her boss (President Nixon) for decades, or the finest, technical brains of those with whom the advisory panel carefully consulted. The chances of finding the truth today are extremely slim; in fact, the chances are probably impossible. Harry Robbins Haldeman died in 1993; Richard Nixon passed away in 1994; Rose Mary Woods did likewise in 2005; and Alexander Haig took his last breaths in 2010. Whether by accident or design, we can be certain of one thing in this strange caper: On September 29, 1973, a major part of American history was erased for good (Ibid.).

Now it's time to address the erasing of a man who played a major role in the decision that ultimately sent troops into Iraq, and also into battle, in 2003.

18: SEVENTY YEARS IN THE MAKING

In the immediate post-9/11 era, and up until 2005, more than two dozen people who worked in the domain of microbiology—which is the study of organisms that are too minute to be seen with the naked eye, such as bacteria and viruses—were found dead under highly dubious circumstances, and all around the world. At first glance, the deaths seemed to be due to wholly natural causes, late-night muggings, and suicides provoked by depression and overwork. That there was such a proliferation of deaths in a clearly defined period and all around the globe, however—and in a field hardly known for being hazardous on such a large scale—raised many red flags. Some of those red flags caused secret, official investigations to be launched by the governments of the United States and the United Kingdom. They were investigations that, in many cases, remain classified and exempt from disclosure to the present day.

As to why, that's easy: More than a few of those same microbiologists had ties to the intelligence agencies of (among others) the United States, Britain, and the former Soviet Union. Unsurprisingly, this curious collection of deaths has led to a multitude of controversial theories to try to rationalize them, including the possibility that Middle Eastern terrorists and assassins are trying to wipe out the leading lights of the Western world's experts in the fields of virology and biological warfare. A far more controversial scenario, suggested by some conspiracy theorists, involved Western agents killing their own people to prevent them from being kidnapped and tortured. The purpose was to ensure any scientists on the kidnappers' list never had the chance to reveal to the enemy their darkest secrets about the current state of exotic viruses that might be employed on the battlefield. Of all those deaths, one stands out more than any other: that of a man named David Kelly, who moved near-effortlessly within the world of British government secrecy. At least he did until he was found dead. To avoid getting ahead of ourselves, however, let's start at the beginning. To do so means taking a trip to a place where the word "virus" has nothing to do with Norton or Kaspersky, but everything to do with disease, death, and classified projects of a biological nature. (We've already come across it in relation to the UFO incident at Rendlesham Forest, Suffolk, England, in December 1980.) It is Porton Down, that closely guarded, near-impenetrable installation where secret research and tinkering are undertaken into the realms of lethal viruses, manufactured diseases, plagues, and biological warfare.

DANGEROUS JOBS, DEATH, AND SEALED FILES

Dr. Vladimir Pasechnik's biggest claim to fame was that he was a leading microbiologist and germ expert for Biopreparat, a major biological weapons company of the former Soviet Union, and that worked hand in glove with the Soviet military and intelligence services. In 1989, while working in Paris, France, Pasechnik—having had enough of life under an iron-fisted regime—fled to the British Embassy, demanding protection and asylum. When he was quickly granted residence in the UK, Pasechnik spilled the biological beans to MI5 and MI6 regarding all he knew about the then current state of viral research in Russia. So pleased and overjoyed was the British government that it decided to offer Pasechnik a job at Porton Down. It was a job that he held down for one year, after which he established his own business, Regma Biotechnics. Things came to a controversial end for Pasechnik on November 21, 2001, when he reportedly died of a stroke. Conveniently for the British government and the staff of Porton Down, shortly before his death, Pasechnik had shared with them all he knew about Soviet research into anthrax. Fortunately for the government, Pasechnik's untimely passing at only 64 meant that he was now unable to tell any other government what he knew about secret Russian research into anthrax. The timing of everything could not have been better. At least, it could not have been better as far as British officialdom was concerned, but certainly not from the unfortunate perspective of Pasechnik.

Equally as controversial as Pasechnik's passing are the things that occurred after his death. Gordon Thomas, a researcher who has studied the Pasechnik

The entrance to Porton Down, Wiltshire, where Dr. David Kelly worked as head of microbiology. ©Nick Redfern

affair, noted: "No details of the autopsy report were made public. While English law demands a coroner's inquest must be open to the public, no prior notice was given to the press of its date or venue. No reporter covered the event. The funeral, which normally would have drawn media attention given who Pasechnik was, went unreported" (Thomas, 2011).

Slightly more than two and a half years later, on July 3, 2004, 52-year-old Dr. Paul Norman, of Salisbury, Wiltshire, England, tragically died when the single-engine Cessna 206 aircraft he was piloting plummeted to the ground in the English county of nearby Devonshire, on land adjacent to the little village of Beacon. It so transpires that Dr. Norman was also the chief scientist for Chemical and Biological Defense at Porton Down. The crash site was quickly closed to the public and a careful analysis of everything was undertaken by officials from the Air Accidents Investigation Branch. The verdict: nothing but a terrible accident. Significant portions of the documentation concerning the incident remain inaccessible to the media and the public. No surprise there.

Between the deaths of Dr. Vladimir Pasechnik in 2001 and Dr. Paul Norman in 2004 came the most controversial death of all. It was that of a certain David Kelly. And just about everyone in the British media, and the general public, too, sat up and took notice when news was announced that the postmortem report on Kelly was going to be sealed, from just about everyone, for no less than 70 years.

THE WMD FIASCO

Dr. David Kelly was a man with a great deal of fingers in many secret and sensitive pies. Back in 1984, Kelly accepted the prestigious position of head of microbiology at Porton Down. Five years later, he was one of the key players involved in debriefing Vladimir Pasechnik, after the latter's defection to the UK. Kelly's role in the debriefing proved to be monumental, as it demonstrated the outrageous extent to which the Soviets had violated protocols concerning the research and development of biological weapons. The debriefing also showed, disturbingly, that the Russians were recklessly dabbling with the Smallpox virus, possibly to try and mutate it into something even worse and then unleash it upon an unsuspecting Western world. Kelly also served as the British Ministry of Defense's chief scientific officer and senior adviser to the proliferation and arms control secretariat, and to the Foreign Office's non-proliferation department. Additionally, he was senior adviser on biological weapons to the United Nations. He had also worked with (but not for, it should be stressed) MI6. It was all going well for Kelly—that is, until the summer of 2003 when matters went from bad to worse and, ultimately, to fatal.

On May 22, 2003, Kelly had an off the record conversation, at London's Charing Cross Hotel, with a reporter from the BBC named Andrew Gilligan. The subject matter was a deeply controversial one. It focused upon a classified British government report of 2002 on the claims that Saddam Hussein was building and stockpiling weapons of mass destruction—weapons that could supposedly be deployed with no more than 45 minutes' notice. Yes, *those* WMDs—the infamous ones that no one was ever able to find, despite repeated claims that they really did exist. The data, recommendations, and conclusions of the report played a major role in bolstering the British government's proclamation that the 2003 invasion of Iraq was of paramount importance from a national security perspective.

For his part, Kelly was profoundly disturbed by the extent of the assertions being made about Iraq's military capabilities at the time. In fact, he was convinced that much of what was said in the report amounted to absolute untruths and that the dossier had been deliberately exaggerated. It's important to note that Kelly *did* suspect that Iraq may well have possessed some WMDs—perhaps ones left over from, but never deployed in, the first Gulf War of 1991. That said, however, he was far from convinced that the people behind the report had their facts straight on the nature or scope of the weapons, and

The British Ministry of Defense: a key player in the David Kelly affair. ©Nick Redfern

particularly so regarding Saddam Hussein's alleged ability to deploy them in significantly less than one hour. Someone, it seems, was doing all they could to ensure that the invasion went ahead, even if it meant exaggerating the data to scare the populace, convince the media, and justify the war.

During their meeting, Kelly made it clear to Andrew Gilligan that nothing he said could be attributed to him by name—*whatsoever*. Gilligan duly agreed to the terms. One week later, the salient points that Kelly made were aired on a BBC show, *Today*. Gilligan noted that the claims suggesting Iraq could deploy WMDs in 45 minutes were, to be as diplomatic as possible, most unlikely. When the show was broadcast, the proverbial you-know-what quickly hit the proverbial fan, and the government of the day angrily demanded to know the name of Gilligan's source.

KELLY'S COVER IS BLOWN

Possibly realizing that eventually, one way or another, his cover would be blown, Kelly decided that the best approach was to come clean with his superiors and reveal to them his side of the story. At least that way Kelly would have some control in how matters developed. Or so he hoped. On June 30th, Kelly contacted his bosses at the Ministry of Defense and explained what had happened during his May 22nd quiet chat with Gilligan. Kelly stressed to the MoD that he was sure he was not Gilligan's main source of the story now causing such a ruckus. True or not, Kelly was most certainly *a* source of information for Gilligan. MoD staff then did something decidedly sneaky: They released a story to the press that confirmed someone had talked out of turn. They did not reveal Kelly's name, but they did disclose enough titbits of data that soon allowed investigative journalists to determine that it was Kelly who was the cause of all the fuss and furor. More outrageously, when those same journalists then approached the MoD with Kelly's name, the MoD confirmed that the press had got the right man. It seems that, whether he was the only source for Andrew Gilligan or not, Kelly was going to become the definitive public enemy number one in the entire saga.

Having been given a formal warning for talking to Gilligan—and not prepared for being thrust into the public eye in such a controversial and graphic fashion, and on a matter that played a significant role in a decision to go to war with Iraq—Kelly's stress levels began to steadily rise. He was ordered to appear twice before the government's House of Commons to answer questions on the Gilligan affair and the role that he had played in it. On one of the two occasions, July 15, 2003, the question-and-answer session was televised for the whole nation to see. No one could deny that Kelly was a man by now living right on the edge. He shakily, and tensely, reiterated the facts. Yes, he *had* spoken to Gilligan but, no, he did not believe that everything that was being attributed to him actually did come from him. Nor did Kelly consider himself to be Gilligan's main source of material. Kelly's words on that memorable day scarcely mattered, however, for only two days later the doctor was no more.

DEATH IN THE WOODS AND A 70-YEAR LOCKDOWN

The morning of July 17th was a busy one for Dr. David Kelly. He was at home in Oxfordshire, replying to e-mails from colleagues and friends who wanted to wish him well at his time of deep trouble. He also received an e-mail from the Ministry of Defense, who wanted to know more about his contacts in the field of journalism and what, exactly, he had said, to whom, and when. Come the afternoon, Kelly, unsurprisingly, wanted a break. Around 3:00 p.m. he decided it was time to get some fresh air. He took a stroll to a nearby area of picturesque woods known locally as Harrowdown Hill. Kelly was not seen alive again. The official story is that he swallowed a considerable number of strong painkillers—29 in total—and sliced into his left wrist with an old knife that he had in his possession since boyhood (a blunt knife, as an examination of it by police showed). Death soon followed. Kelly's body was found, after his wife reported him missing, the following morning.

In the immediate wake of Kelly's death, Tony Blair, the British prime minister at the time, established what was termed the Hutton Inquiry. It was designed to get to the bottom of the matter of Kelly's passing and took its name from the man who oversaw the inquiry, James Brian Edward Hutton, otherwise known as Baron Hutton. Suicide was the unsurprising verdict that was issued on January 28, 2004, with death reportedly resulting from (a) hemorrhaging provoked by wounds to Kelly's left wrist, (b) the large amount of painkillers in his system, and (c) coronary artery atherosclerosis, from which the autopsy reportedly showed he had been suffering.

Many might have been inclined to accept the suicide verdict were it not for one significant factor. Hutton took it upon himself to ensure that the postmortem report, all surrounding medical files, photographs of the body at the site, and records provided but not produced in evidence, should remain behind closed doors for a stunning *seven decades*. Norman Baker, a Liberal Democrat Member of Parliament, who was highly suspicious of the conclusion that Kelly had committed suicide, was amazed and near-dumbstruck by the decision, as were millions of other Britons.

BLOOD: MISSING FROM THE SCENE

In the wake of Lord Hutton's conclusions and his decision to deny access to the material evidence, deep suspicions were aired suggesting that Kelly's death was not the result of an act born out of desperation, anxiety, and depression. Take, for example, the story of Vanessa Hunt and Dave Bartlett. Their testimony is of paramount importance, as they were the first paramedics on the scene after Kelly's body was found in the woods. Because significant blood loss from the cut to Kelly's wrist was reported to be a major factor that led to his death, it's intriguing that Hunt and Bartlett both vocally commented on the extraordinary *lack* of blood at the scene. This made a mockery of Lord Hutton, who wrote in his report: "It is my opinion that the main factor involved in bringing about the death of David Kelly is the bleeding from the incised wounds to his left wrist. Had this not occurred he may well not have died at this time" (Taylor, 2010).

In reality, aside from a tiny amount of blood that was found on nearby plants, and a patch of blood no bigger than a small coin on the clothes of Kelly, there was no spilled blood in evidence anywhere. And remember: The wound to Kelly's wrist was said to have been no slight, half-hearted cut born out of a cry for help. The knife had reportedly sliced into an artery. The artery in question was the ulnar artery, which is the chief blood vessel of the forearm. As experienced paramedics, all of this left Hunt and Bartlett profoundly puzzled and surprised by what they found at the scene—or, rather, what they didn't find: much in the way of blood. As we'll see later, blood may well have been spilled, after all. But it may have been washed away by certain government people before Vanessa Hunt and Dave Bartlett were even on the scene. And blood wasn't the only thing missing from the scene of David Kelly's death.

FINGERPRINTS AND DNA: ALSO MISSING

In October 2007, thanks to documentation that surfaced under the terms of the Freedom of Information Act, a baffling and disturbing revelation was made. The knife that was used to slice into Kelly's artery was totally lacking in fingerprints. But that's not all. Kelly's glasses, his cell phone, a water bottle, and the packet that contained the co-proxamol pills that Kelly swallowed (or that he was forced to swallow) were also completely clean of prints. Why Kelly would have wanted to carefully wipe every single print off of every one of the above items is a mystery that still lingers on to this day. Unless, of course, Kelly wasn't the person who carefully wiped them all clean. Some might say that perhaps Kelly was wearing gloves at the time. Then, having wiped the items clean, he left no further prints on them. That would be fine, except for one glaring issue: Kelly was not wearing gloves when he left the house the day before his body was found, and no gloves were found on his hands, near his body, or anywhere at the scene.

If the absent blood and fingerprints weren't enough to convince people that Kelly had been murdered, the next revelation certainly changed the minds of many. Kelly's glasses, which he routinely wore, lacked any signs of telltale DNA. Glasses, which fit snuggly against the skin of the wearer, should be teeming with minute DNA. Not with Kelly's glasses, though. The cleaning of the glasses had been achieved to such an incredible extent that not even *one* microscopic DNA cell could be found anywhere on what was, without doubt, an item that Kelly used every day of his life.

A HARD DRIVE GETS WIPED

One man who was determined to get to the bottom of the many controversies surrounding the death of David Kelly was the British government's member of Parliament for Lewes, Scotland, the aforementioned Norman Baker. He noted in 2006: "What my investigations to date have demonstrated is that there are significant medical doubts from professional medical people about the alleged cause of death...I am suggesting explanation for suicide doesn't add up" ("Files 'Wiped' in Dr Kelly Inquiry," 2006).

Deeply suspiciously, and at the height of Baker's probe, the hard drive of his computer was wiped clean of the files that he, Baker, had compiled on Kelly's death. Fortunately, Baker was not deterred by this action which he suspected had probably been achieved remotely. The culprit was never identified or found. In 2007, Baker's book on the matter, *The Strange Death of David Kelly*, was published, and was prominently serialized in one of the UK's most popular, nationally available newspapers, the *Daily Mail*. So, if murder *was* the cause of Kelly's death, then who might have been the guilty parties behind it?

HIT LISTS AND EXTERMINATION

One of those who commented on the possibility that someone was out to get Kelly and take him out of action (permanently) was Richard O. Spertzel. A noted authority in the fields of biological warfare and microbiology, Spertzel, between 1994 and 1998, held the position of senior biologist for the United Nations Special Commission that was charged with monitoring and inspecting the activities of the Iraqis, to ensure they were not secretly working to create WMDs. Spertzel also had significant input in germ warfare studies undertaken at the U.S. equivalent of Porton Down: Fort Detrick, which is located in Maryland.

Spertzel said, in June 2010: "I know that David, as well as myself and a couple of others, were on an Iraqi hit-list. In late 1997, we were told by the Russian embassy in Baghdad. I had no idea what it meant but apparently David and I were high on the priority list." He continued, surely echoing what much of the British public and the nation's media thought too: "It just doesn't make sense. It seems to me that [the British government] are intentionally ignoring all this" (Goslett and Martin, 2010).

Another source who commented on such matters was a former KGB agent named Boris Karpichkov. He made no bones about the situation, asserting, only a month after the words of Richard O. Spertzel hit the newswires, that Kelly had been terminated. Karpichkov, who defected to the UK in 1998 after spending a decade and a half with the KGB, said his source was an intelligence operative with links to MI5. Karpichkov's story was one full of the kind of twists and turns one might expect to see in a high-tech, Hollywood conspiracy-based thriller.

Karpichkov claimed that his source was a man named Peter Everett. Until 2006, Everett had run a London-based company called Group Global Intelligence Services, which utilized the skills of former MI5 personnel. Karpichkov said that he had worked for Everett, and that the pair had met on many occasions. One of those occasions was only two days after David Kelly's death. The former KGB spy maintained that Everett told him how the circumstances surrounding Kelly's death were highly suspicious, as was the fact that the first law enforcement people on the scene were not the local police, but members of Special Branch, an elite arm of the British Police Force whose work focuses to a high degree on counter-terrorism.

Karpichkov further maintained that Everett told him the Special Branch team moved Kelly's body from its original location, altered the positioning of his body, and removed all incriminating data. Who the data incriminated, and why, was not made apparent. Moreover, adding to the controversy concerning the lack of fingerprints on the various items at the scene—such as on Kelly's water bottle and glasses—Karpichkov said he was advised by Everett that the scene of the crime was thoroughly cleaned of any evidence, including prints. Maybe that wash-out was responsible for the complete lack of any microscopic-sized DNA cells on Kelly's glasses.

Controversially, when Karpichkov inquired as to what might have prompted the need to have David Kelly killed, he claims that the answer received from Everett did not point in the direction of Iraq. Rather, Karpichkov said that Everett did not reply in direct terms, but suggested that the guilty parties were attached to the competition. In Karpichkov's mind, this was a reference to MI6, because MI5 and MI6 are known to have had a strained relationship on many occasions over the decades. But why might British Intelligence have wanted Kelly dead? The Russian suggested that it was due to the doctor's recent actions, such as speaking with BBC journalist Andrew Gilligan.

As for Peter Everett, when approached by the British media for his side of the story, he admitted that he knew Karpichkov, and confirmed he had spoken with him on the matter of Kelly's death. Everett flatly denied, however, having access to any insider information. He refused to comment on allegations that he had worked for MI5, but did concede that he had spent an undisclosed number of years employed in the realm of intelligence.

The words of Boris Karpichkov and Richard O. Spertzel, the publication of Norman Baker's book (*The Strange Death of David Kelly*), and overall media and public skepticism concerning the controversial circumstances surrounding Kelly's supposed suicide, led to a remarkable development in late 2010.

DOCUMENTATION FINALLY SURFACES

In October 2010, as the controversy surrounding the death of David Kelly showed no signs of going away in the near future, there was a surprising move in the case. The 14-page postmortem, which had been locked away in 2004 for 70 years, was finally made public. It may not be a coincidence that the release of the material, by government officials, came specifically *after* the May 6, 2010 general election, which saw the return of a conservative government to the United Kingdom. It was under the previous labor government that the postmortem had been classified, and it was the labor government that had expressed so much displeasure regarding David Kelly's interview with the BBC's Andrew Gilligan. Perhaps this was an example of the Conservative government sending a message to Labor that it was not happy with the near-Orwellian situation of denying everyone access to the postmortem for seven decades. On its release, Lord Sutton was quick to play down the angle that the report—and the accompanying six-page toxicology report, which had also been classified for 70 years—had been withheld for reasons of cover-up or conspiracy. Nor, Sutton said, had there been any kind of attempt to hide anything. Instead, Sutton maintained that his actions were primarily prompted out of respect and concern for the family of David Kelly.

The release of the postmortem was welcome, but in the end, it didn't change anything. Questions and controversies continued (and still continue) to surround such matters as the lack of blood at the site, the near-unfathomable absence of any DNA samples on Kelly's glasses, the missing fingerprints, claims of MI6 complicity in Kelly's death, Norman Baker's wiped computer, allegations that Special Branch officers rearranged the scene in the woods and engaged in a major cleanup operation, and the statements of Richard O. Spertzel and Boris Karpichkov that Kelly had been targeted for death, whether by the Iraqis or by MI6.

We may never fully know what really happened on July 17, 2003, in the Harrowdown Hill woods. But of one thing we can be fairly sure: Someone seemingly covered their tracks very well. That's hardly surprising, however, in a world where someone can casually classify a significant medical document for 70 years.

CONCLUSION

Our quest to seek out the truth of many strange and conspiratorial sagas relative to missing files, vanished documents, sealed records, and denied papers is now at its end. That means it's time to try to make some sense of (a) the entire situation of secrecy within the realm of officialdom, and (b) how and why documents get hidden, destroyed, or denied release. We'll begin with the CIA's mind control-themed operation, Project MKUltra. Yes, a massive percentage of the MKUltra material was shredded and burned. But it was clearly something of which not everyone in the CIA approved, and that was done, primarily, to protect Richard Helms. Thus, destruction is not always down to "the government," but to single figures working within the official infrastructure.

Turning our attention toward the quest to try to resolve the matter of the missing records on the notorious UFO-themed affair at Roswell, New Mexico in July 1947, we see a somewhat different situation. The lack of files on Roswell may be due to the case falling under the near-impenetrable auspices of one of those classified SAPs (Special Access Programs), to which entrance can only be gained by having the necessary, highly-classified coded data. It's likely that the events that occurred in the heart of Rendlesham Forest in December 1980—suggesting that aliens may well have visited the United Kingdom over the course of three nights—is also protected by SAP-type legislation.

Let's now focus on those famous faces that have attracted so much secret attention. We'll start with the late Diana, Princess of Wales and the Squidgygate affair. A good guess can be made that the original phone recordings between James Gilbey and Diana were probably destroyed to hide a sensational fact: there were people in British Intelligence trying to undermine, and destroy the credibility of, the mother to the heir of the British throne. As far as that other famous blond was concerned—Marilyn Monroe—it wasn't so much for who she was that got the CIA in a whirl, and that has led to a consistent, unswerving denial that the agency possesses any files on the famous actress. Instead, it was her associations. Actually, two key associations: those with President John F. Kennedy, and his brother, Robert, the Attorney General under the JFK administration. Keeping the lid on the full facts of those relationships was, and perhaps still is, paramount.

On those highly controversial matters of the CIA's Operation Often, it's not hard to fathom why the agency will neither confirm nor deny the existence of the program. Perhaps, in a God-fearing nation like the United States, officialdom is concerned about the public backlash that would likely be provoked by an announcement that one of the most powerful agencies in the world was dabbling into such issues as Satanism, occult ritual, and witchcraft. Similar concerns may explain MI5's decision to not reveal anything of significance on occultist Aleister Crowley.

In many respects, the matters of the withheld material on the JFK assassination of November 1963, the destruction of J. Edgar Hoover's voluminous secret files after his death on May 2, 1972, President Nixon's infamous erased phone call of June 20, 1972, and the massive amount of missing files identified, in 1994, by President Bill Clinton's Advisory Committee on Human Radiation Experiments, may all have had personal agendas at their hearts.

Nixon's actions were the result of the man trying, desperately and near-singlehandedly, to cling on to his presidency, but ultimately and spectacularly failing. Hoover's secretary, Helen Gandy, was dutifully abiding by the directives of her late boss. If a wide-reaching conspiracy was indeed at the heart of President Kennedy's death, then the decision to withhold or destroy papers may have been born out of fear. It could be fear among the final few old-timers in officialdom who know the truth that something still exists, something that, more than half a century later, could still blow the whole issue wide open. As for the investigations undertaken by the Advisory Committee on Human Radiation Experiments, one suspects that far more than a few figures who played direct roles in the experiments would have had vested interests in destroying certain records, if they feared them ever reaching the public.

It might seem strange to link the matter of a secret space program—one under classified military control, rather than run openly by government—with the death of Dr. David Kelly, the biological warfare expert found dead under controversial circumstances in 2003. But there is a connection: the furthering of military goals and ambitions. Regarding the secret space program, if such a thing does exist, then those within the military who oversee it may have saturated it in secrecy, and hidden and denied files, to ensure that their agenda of outer space–based expansion and domination can proceed without interference and scrutiny.

So what is the connection to Dr. David Kelly? Military agendas, that's what. Dr. Kelly was a very intelligent man, a figure deeply respected in his field of research, and someone whose word could be relied upon. So, when he began complaining loudly that the British government's report on Saddam Hussein's elusive weapons of mass destruction had been significantly exaggerated, he suddenly became someone who had the real ability to reign in the government's goals and ambitions in Iraq. That is, until his sudden death conveniently intervened.

What we have, then, are events, circumstances, and situations where people and agencies of government, the military, and the world of intelligence have taken it upon themselves to withhold from the general public what is clearly a truly massive body of official documentation of the highest classification. And on occasion, when fears exist that just withholding files that may affect national security isn't enough, the material has been relegated to the furnace and the shredder.

So much for the past; what does the future hold for us on the matter of denied and missing files? In all probability, the trends of years gone by will continue to dominate the years ahead. A perfect example is the case of Edward Snowden. He is the National Security Agency (and former CIA) employee who, in early 2013, blew the whistle on the NSA's massive program to collect data on the phone calls, e-mails, and social networking habits of American citizens. When Britain's *Guardian* newspaper revealed the shocking extent to which the NSA's Tempora and PRISM programs had the populace under surveillance, the revelations provoked widespread condemnation and outrage across the United States.

The Obama administration, and the NSA, responded by stating that officialdom was not voyeuristically trawling through millions upon millions of private e-mails, or transcribing every phone call under the sun. Rather, it was simply collecting phone numbers and data, and looking for threads and leads that might prevent terrorist attacks on the United States. Much of the criticism of the NSA's programs stemmed from the fact that the government refused to release any hard data—in the form of documentation—to demonstrate how, precisely, terrorist activity had been curtailed by watching America. Yes, there have been significant successes, said officialdom, but, no, you can't see the files that explain those successes. And, so far, we still have not.

The Snowden revelations led to another development, one that has been seldom discussed and highlighted, but that demonstrates it's not just the general public that is denied access to the full facts of the controversy. In late June 2013, the U.S. Army confirmed that it had taken steps to specifically prevent thousands of personnel in the Department of Defense from accessing portions of the *Guardian's* Website. The military described its actions as "network hygiene," designed to ensure that classified data did not appear on DoD networks that were unclassified (Ackerman and Roberts, 2013).

Thus, in the electronic age, we see a new and disturbing way in which data is withheld. Not by shredding or burning it, but by actively preventing people from accessing it on the Internet. Will we, in the years and decades to come, see further examples of censorship of the Internet? In all probability, that will depend on the specific nature of future world events. Of one thing, however, we can be sure: When government agencies relegate files, records, and even portions of the *Guardian's* Website to that secret domain stamped *For Nobody's Eyes Only*, they really do mean exactly that.

BIBLIOGRAPHY

Ackerman, Spencer, and Dan Roberts. "US Army Blocks Access to Guardian Website to Preserve 'Network Hygiene.'" *www.guardian.co.uk/world/2013/jun/28/us-army-blocks-guardian-website-access.* June 28, 2013.

Advisory Committee on Human Radiation Experiments: Final Report. Washington, D.C.: U.S. Government Printing Office, 1995.

Alford, Matthew. "CIA Responds to Ex-Official's 'Roswell Happened' Claim: Not True."*http://silverscreensaucers.blogspot.com/2012/07/cia-responds-to-ex-officials-roswell.html.* July 11, 2012.

Allen, Nick, and Gordon Rayner. "Diana's Squidgygate Tapes 'Leaked by GCHQ.'" *www.telegraph.co.uk/news/uknews/1575117/Dianas-Squidgygate-tapes-leaked-by-GCHQ.html.* January 9, 2008.

"Andrew Gilligan: I Did Not Betray David Kelly or Reveal Him as My Source." *www.guardian.co.uk/theobserver/2010/aug/29/david-kelly-nick-cohen-andrew-gilligan.* August 28, 2010.

Angelucci, Orfeo, and Timothy Green Beckley (editor). *Son of the Sun: Secret of the Saucers.* New Brunswick, N.J.: Inner Light, 2008.

"Army Ropes off Area: Unidentified Flying Object Falls near Kecksburg," *Tribune-Review*, December 10, 1965.

Apiryon, T. "Doctor (Albert Karl) Theodor Reuss." *http://hermetic.com/sabazius/reuss.htm.* 1999.

"Australia UFO Sighting Files Mysteriously Disappear." *www.huffingtonpost.com/2011/06/07/australia-ufo-sighting-files-disappear-_n_872543.html.* June 7, 2011.

Ayton, Mel. "The 'Assassination' of Marilyn Monroe." *www.crimemagazine.com/05/marilynmonroe,0724-5.htm.* July 24, 2005.

Bach, Lord. "Memorandum." October 13, 2012.

Baker, Norman. *The Strange Death of David Kelly.* York, U.K.: Methuen Publishing. Ltd., 2007.

———. "Why I know weapons expert Dr David Kelly was murdered, by the MP who spent a year investigating his death." *www.dailymail.co.uk/news/article-488667/Why-I-know-weapons-expert-Dr-David-Kelly-murdered-MP-spent-year-investigating-death.html.* October 20, 2007.

Bardsley, Marilyn. "The Life and Career of J. Edgar Hoover." *www.trutv.com/library/crime/gangsters_outlaws/cops_others/hoover/2.html.* 2013.

Bassam, Lord of Brighton. "Memorandum." January 27, 2002.

Batty, David, "New Medical Evidence Could Stop Hacker Gary McKinnon's Extradition." *www.guardian.co.uk/world/2009/oct/26/garry-mckinnon-extradition-alan-johnson.* October 26, 2009.

Bell, Rachel. "The Death of Marilyn Monroe." *www.trutv.com/library/crime/notorious_murders/celebrity/marilyn_monroe/index.html.* 2013.

Berlitz, Charles, and William L. Moore. *The Roswell Incident.* London, U.K.: Granada Publishing Ltd., 1980.

Bernstein, Carl, and Bob Woodward. *All the President's Men.* New York: Simon & Schuster, 1994.

Besser, Linton. "Alien abduction? Defense's X-Files are lost in space." *www.smh.com.au/technology/sci-tech/alien-abduction-defences-xfiles-are-lost-in-space-20110606-1fpea.html.* June 7, 2011.

Bishop, Greg. *Wake Up Down There!* Kempton, Ill.: Adventures Unlimited Press, 2000.

Blake, Ian. "Aleister Crowley and the Lam Statement." *www.excludedmiddle.com/LAM statement.html.* 1996.

"Blundeston Prison Information." *www.justice.gov.uk/contacts/prison-finder/blundeston.* April 22, 2013.

Botham, Noel. *The Murder of Princess Diana.* Wellington, New Zealand: Pinnacle, 2004.

Booth, Martin. *A Magick Life: The Life of Aleister Crowley.* Philadelphia, Penn.: Coronet Books, 2000.

Borland, Ben, "David Cameron Can Save Hacker From US Jail Hell." *www.dailyexpress.co.uk/posts/view/180683/David-Cameron-CAN-save-hacker-from-U-S-Jail-hell/.* June 13, 2010.

Bruni, Georgina. "Admiral Lord Hill-Norton." *www.therendleshamforestincident.com/Admiral_Lord_Hill-Norton.html.* 2013.

Bruni, Georgina. *You Can't Tell the People.* London, U.K.: Macmillan, 2001.

Bull, John. "The Wickedest Man in the World." *Sunday Express*, March 24, 1923.

Carter, John. *Sex and Rockets: The Occult World of Jack Parsons.* Port Townsend, Wash.: Feral House, 1999.

Claiborne, William. "GAO Investigating Report That Government Covered Up '47 UFO Incident." *Washington Post*, January 30, 1994.

Clarke, David. "The Secret Files: The Cosford Incident." *www.uk-ufo.org/condign/secfilcosf2.htm.* 2005.

Cleaver, A. V. "'Electro-gravitics': What it is—or might be." *Journal of the British Interplanetary Society*, April–June, 1957.

"CNN Larry King Live." *http://transcripts.cnn.com/TRANSCRIPTS/0307/01/lkl.00. html.* July 1, 2003.

Cobb, Michael. "How to apply government data classification standards to your company." *www.computerweekly.com/news/1355736/How-to-apply-government-data-clas sification-standards-to-your-company.* May 6, 2009.

Cork, John. "The Life of Ian Fleming (1908–1964)." *www.klast.net/bond/flem_bio.html.* 1995.

Corso, Philip, and William Birnes. *The Day after Roswell.* New York: Simon & Schuster, 1997.

Corydon, Bent, and L. Ron Hubbard, Jr. *L. Ron Hubbard: Messiah or Madman?* Secaucus, N.J.: Lyle Stuart Inc., 1987.

Covert, Norman. "A History of Fort Detrick, Maryland." *www.detrick.army.mil/cut ting_edge/index.cfm.* October 2000.

Davidson, Michael, and Michael C. Ruppert. "A Career in Microbiology can be Harmful to Your Health." *www.fromthewilderness.com/free/ww3/02_14_02_microbio.html.* February, 14, 2002.

Defense Intelligence Agency document (title deleted according to FOIA regulations), September 22, 1976.

Department of the Air Force, *AFCIN Intelligence Team Personnel*, November 3, 1961.

Dolan, Richard M. "Musings on a Secret Space Program." *http://richardthomasblogger. blogspot.com/.* June 6, 2010.

Doward, Jamie. "Top secret US files could hold clues to death of Diana." *www.guardian. co.uk/uk/2004/jan/11/monarchy.jamiedoward.* January 10, 2004.

Doyle, Patricia. "More Dead Top Microbiologist Scientists." *www.rense.com/general48/ moredead.htm.* January 29, 2004.

"Dr. David Kelly: Controversial death examined." *www.bbc.co.uk/news/uk-13716127.* December 17, 2011.

Dudurich, Ann Saul. "Kecksburg UFO Debate Renewed." *www.PittsburghLive.com.* August 3, 2003.

"Eavesdropper Regrets Selling Tape Of Diana." *www.deseretnews.com/article/246831/ EAVESDROPPER-REGRETS-SELLING-TAPE-OF-DIANA.html?pg=all.* September 10, 1992.

"The EOB Tape of June 20, 1972." *www.aes.org/aeshc/docs/forensic.audio/watergate. tapes.report.pdf.* 2013.

Evans, Michael. "Porton Down guinea-pigs get apology." *Sunday Times*, January 18, 2008.

"Executive Order 13526 Classified National Security Information." *www.whitehouse.gov/the- press-office/executive-order-classified-national-security-information.* December 29, 2009.

Fawcett, Lawrence, and Barry J. Greenwood. *Clear Intent: The Government Cover-Up of the UFO Experience.* Englewood Cliffs, N.J.: Prentice-Hall, Inc., 1984.

"FBI Adds New Subjects to Electronic Reading Room." *http://cryptome.org/fbi-spies. htm.* March 2, 2000.

"FBI Records: The Vault." *http://vault.fbi.gov/.* April 1, 2011.

Federal Bureau of Investigation document on Kenneth Goff, November 5 1951.

"Files 'wiped' in Dr Kelly inquiry." *http://news.bbc.co.uk/2/hi/uk_news/england/south ern_counties/5178302.stm.* July 13, 2006.

"Fireball a Meteor, Astronomer Explains." *Pittsburgh Post-Gazette*, December 10, 1965.

"The FOIA and President Lyndon Johnson." *www.gwu.edu/~nsarchiv/nsa/foia/lbj.html*. 2013.

Fuller, Jean Overton. *The Magical Dilemma of Victor Neuberg*. Oxford, U.K.: Mandrake, 2005.

Galvin, Rachel. "Arthur Miller Biography." *www.neh.gov/about/awards/jefferson-lecture/arthur-miller-biography*. 2013.

General Accounting Office. *Results of a Search for Records Concerning the 1947 Crash Near Roswell, New Mexico*. July 28, 1995.

Gentry, Curt. *J. Edgar Hoover: The Man and His Secrets*. New York: W.W. Norton & Company, 2001.

Goslett, Miles, and Arthur Martin. "Dr. David Kelly was on a hitlist, says UN weapons expert as Calls grow for full inquest." *www.dailymail.co.uk/news/article-1302939/Dr-David-Kelly-hitlist-says-UN-weapons-expert-calls-grow-inquest.html*. August 13, 2010.

Goff, Kenneth. *Red Shadows*. Fort Worth, Tx.: Manney Company, 1959.

Gordon, Stan. "Stan Gordon's UFO Anomalies Zone: Kecksburg UFO Crash." *www.stangordonufo.com/kecksburg/kecksburg%20home.htm*. 2009.

———. "The Kecksburg Incident: An Updated Review." *1st Annual UFO Crash Retrieval Conference Proceedings*. Broomfield, Colo.: Wood & Wood Enterprises, 2003.

Gorightly, Adam. "Ritual Magic, Mind Control and the UFO Phenomenon." *www.conspiracyarchive.com/UFOs/UFO_Ritual_Magic.htm*. 2001.

Goslett, Miles. "David Kelly post mortem to be kept secret for 70 years as doctors accuse Lord Hutton of concealing vital information." *www.dailymail.co.uk/news/article-1245599/David-Kelly-post-mortem-kept-secret-70-years-doctors-accuse-Lord-Hutton-concealing-vital-information.html*. January 25, 2010.

———. "Police admit they could not find trace of fingerprints on Dr David Kelly's glasses after 'suicide.'" *www.dailymail.co.uk/news/article-1366301/David-Kelly-inquest-Police-admit-fingerprints-DNA-glasses.html*. March 14, 2011.

Greenwald, Glenn, Ewen MacAskill, and Laura Poitras. "Edward Snowden: the whistle blower behind the NSA surveillance revelations." *www.guardian.co.uk/world/2013/jun/09/edward-snowden-nsa-whistleblower-surveillance#start-of-comments*. June 10, 2013.

Gregory, Adela, and Milo Speriglio. *Crypt 33: The Saga of Marilyn Monroe—The Final Word*. Secaucus, N.J.: Carol Publishing Corporation, 1993.

"Hacker Feels US Navy Has Spaceships, Crews In Space." *http://rense.com/general67/hackerfeelsUSnavyhas.htm*. July 15, 2005.

Halt, Colonel Charles. Memorandum to the British Ministry of Defense. January 13, 1981.

———. Statement made at *UFO Magazine* lecture. Leeds, England, July 31, 1994.

Harris, Paul, and Tom Kelly. "Queen's fury at 'Squidgygate' tape." *www.dailymail.co.uk/news/article-507163/Queens-fury-Squidgygate-tape-Palace-ordered-inquiry-leaked-Diana-lover.html*. January 10, 2008.

Hecklerspary staff. "Who Killed Marilyn Monroe? Bobby Kennedy, Says New Book." *www.hecklerspray.com/who-killed-marilyn-monroe/200814531.php*. June 4, 2008.

Henderson, Neil. "UFO files reveal 'Rendlesham incident' papers missing." *www.bbc.co.uk/news/uk-12613690*. March 2, 2011.

"Highpoint prison visiting information." *www.justice.gov.uk/contacts/prison-finder/highpoint-south/visiting-information*. April 19, 2013.

Hill-Norton, Lord. Letter to the British Ministry of Defense, September 24, 2002.

———. Memorandum, January 11, 2001.

———. Memorandum, January 12, 2001.

———. Memorandum, January 23, 2001.

———. Memorandum, October 23, 1997.

"HMS Manchester." *www.royalnavy.mod.uk/The-Fleet/Ships/Decommissioned-Units/HMS-Manchester*. 2013.

"Hollesley Bay." *www.justice.gov.uk/contacts/prison-finder/hollesley-bay*. March 5, 2012.

Hollingsworth, Mark, and Nick Fielding. *Defending the Realm: MI5 and the Shayler Affair*. London, U.K.: Andre Deutsch Ltd., 1999.

Howard, Michael. "The British Occult Secret Service—The Untold Story." *New Dawn Magazine*. 107 March–April 2008.

Humphreys, Richard. "Dennis Wheatley: An Introduction." *www.denniswheatley.info/denniswheatley.htm*. 2002.

"I Saw Structures on the Moon (Karl Wolfe)." *www.ufocasebook.com/moonstructures.html*. Undated.

"Ingo Swann Gets Feedback Regarding Naked Men on the Moon." *http://archive.alienzoo.com/conspiracytheory/ingoswann.html*. April 27, 2000.

"Ingo Swann-Penetration, The Moon Remotely Viewed." *www.abovetopsecret.com/forum/thread505569/pg1*. September 28, 2009.

Introvigne, Massimo. "L. Ron Hubbard, Kenneth Goff, And The 'Brain-Washing Manual Of 1955." *www.cesnur.org/2005/brainwash_13.htm*. 2013.

"John Edgar Hoover." *www.fbi.gov/about-us/history/directors/hoover*. 2013.

"John Kiriakou." *www.rollingstone.com/politics/lists/the-new-political-prisoners-leakers-hackers-and-activists-20130301/john-kiriakou-19691231*. 2013.

Jones, M.A. FBI memorandum to Cartha DeLoach. February 11, 1965.

"Judgments McKinnon V Government of the United States of America and Another, House of Lords." *www.publications.parliament.uk/pa ld200708/ldjudgmt/jd080730/mckinn-1.htm*. July 30, 2008.

Kean, Leslie. "Forty Years of Secrecy: NASA, the Military, and the 1965 Kecksburg Crash." *International UFO Reporter*, Vol. 30, No. 1.

———. "Project Moon Dust and Operation Blue Fly: The Retrieval of Objects of Unknown Origin." *www.bibliotecapleyades.net/sociopolitica/esp_sociopol_mj12_3k.htm*. 2002.

———. "The Conclusion of the NASA Lawsuit Concerning the Kecksburg, PA UFO Case of 1965." *www.freedomofinfo.org/foi/NASA_lawsuit_conclusion.pdf*. November 2009.

———. "The Cosmos 96 Question is Settled Once and for All." *www.freedomofinfo.org/news/cosmos-96.pdf*. October, 2003.

Keyhoe, Donald E. *Aliens from Space*. New York: New American Library, 1974.

Kilgallen, Dorothy. "Flying Saucer News." *Los Angeles Examiner*, May 23, 1955.

King, Jon. "US Prosecution of Gary McKinnon 'Spiteful' Says Ex-Top Cop." *www.con sciousape.com/news/us-prosecution-of-gary-mckinnon-spiteful-says-ex-top-cop/*. May 10, 2010.

King, Jon, and John Beveridge. *Princess Diana: The Hidden Evidence*. New York: S.P.I. Books, 2001.

Kirk, Jeremy. "Security Advice from a Wanted Hacker." *PC World. www.pcworld.com/ article/125584/security_advice_from_a_wanted_hacker.html*. April 27, 2006.

Kominksy, Morris. *The Hoaxers: Plain Liars, Fancy Liars, and Damned Liars*. Wellesley, Mass.: Branden Books, 1970.

Kress, Dr. Kenneth A. "Parapsychology in Intelligence." *Studies in Intelligence*. Langley, Va.: Central Intelligence Agency, winter 1977.

"Kuji Media Corporation: The History of a Computer Hacker." *www.kujimedia.com/*. 2007.

Lammer, Helmutt, and Marion Lammer. *MILABS: Military Mind Control & Alien Abduction*. Atlanta, Ga.: IllumiNet Press, 1999.

Langley, William. "The Mannakee File." *www.telegraph.co.uk/news/uknews/1478804/ The-Mannakee-file.html*. December 12, 2004.

Lawrence, Rick. "Helen W. Gandy." *www.findagrave.com/cgibin/fg.cgi?page=gr&GRid =80452994*. November 14, 2011.

Lendman, Stephen. "MK-Ultra—The CIA's Mind Control Program." *http://rense.com/ general89/mkultra.htm*. February 16, 2010.

Leonard, George. *Somebody Else is on the Moon*. New York: Pocket, 1977.

"Louis Patrick Gray III." *www.fbi.gov/about-us/history/directors/gray*. 2013.

Luscombe, Richard. "NASA Told to Solve 'UFO Crash' X-File," *Observer*, November 11, 2007.

Mandelbaum, W. Adam. *The Psychic Battlefield: A History of the Military-Occult Complex*. New York: St. Martin's Griffin, 2002.

"Marilyn Monroe." *http://vault.fbi.gov/Marilyn%20Monroe*. 2013.

"The Marilyn Monroe CIA Memo." *www.blackmesapress.com/page4.htm*. 2013

Marrs, Jim. *Crossfire: The Plot that Killed Kennedy*. New York: Carroll & Graf Publishers, 1989.

McAndrew, Captain James. *The Roswell Report: Case Closed*. Headquarters United States Air Force, 1997.

Mellinger, Philip T. "Cracking Watergate's Infamous 18½ Minute Gap." *www.forensic mag.com/article/cracking-watergates-infamous-18-12-minute-gap*. February 18, 2011.

"The Ministry of Information, INF Series and INF 3." *www.nationalarchives.gov.uk/ theartofwar/inf3.htm*. 2013.

Moore, Charles. "A vast, loyal band of working-class Conservatives." *www.telegraph. co.uk/comment/columnists/charlesmoore/7983677/A-vast-loyal-band-of-working-class-Conservatives.html*. September 6, 2010.

"NASA to Search Files on '65 UFO Incident." *www.msnbc.msn.com/id/21494221/*. October 26, 2007.

"National Archives Decides to Withhold Records Related to the Assassination of President John F. Kennedy." *www.aarclibrary.org/notices/AARC_PressRe lease_2012-06-12.pdf*. June 12, 2012.

"The New Roswell: Kecksburg Exposed." SyFy Channel, 2003.

"The 1973 Fire, National Personnel Records Center." *www.archives.gov/st-louis/mili tary-personnel/fire-1973.html*. 2013.

Noyes, Ralph. *A Secret Property*. London, U.K.: Quartet Books, 1986.

"Official Secrets Act 1989." *www.legislation.gov.uk/ukpga/1989/6/contents*. 2013.

Ong, Cara. "Human Nuclear Experiments." *www.nuclearfiles.org/menu/key-issues/eth ics/issues/scientific/human-nuclear-experiments.htm*. 2013.

"Operation Often: Satanism in the CIA." *http://coverthistory.blogspot.com/2007/12/ operation-often-satanism-in-cia-this.html*. December 17, 2007.

Pacheco, Nelson S., and Tommy R. Blann. *Unmasking the Enemy: Visions Around the World and Global Deception in the End Times*. Arlington, Va.: Bendan Press, Inc., 1993.

Padbury, Wendy. *The Plague Makers*. London, U.K.: Vision Paperbacks, 2002.

"PEN International." *www.pen-international.org/*. 2013.

Pike, John. "Mystery Aircraft: Aurora/Senior Citizen." *www.fas.org/irp/mystery/aurora. htm*. July 24, 1998.

———. "Pine Gap, Australia." *www.fas.org/irp/facility/pine_gap.htm*. October 20, 1999.

Pilkington, Ed. "Manning judge trial to U.S.: prove suspect new leaks would 'aid enemy.'" *www.guardian.co.uk/world/2013/apr/10/bradley-manning-tria wikileaks-suspect*. April 10, 2013.

"Pilot may have caused fatal plane crash by switching to empty fuel tank." *www.dai lymail.co.uk/news/article-471827/Pilot-caused-fatal-plane-crash-switching-fuel-tank.html*. August 3, 2007.

Pope, Nick. "The Cosford Incident." *www.nickpope.net/cosford-incident.htm*. Undated.

"Porton Down." *http://webarchive.nationalarchives.gov.uk/+/http://www.mod.uk/ Defence Internet/AboutDefence/WhatWeDo/HealthandSafety/PortonDownVol unteers/PortonDown.htm*. Undated.

"Porton Down—The Unwitting Victims." *www.bbc.co.uk/insideout/west/series1/por ton-down.shtml*. October 28, 2002.

Powell, Michael. "Evidence of UFO Encounter with HMS Manchester 'lost.'" *www.portsmouth.co.uk/news/local/evidence-of-ufo-encounter-with-hms-man chester-lost-1-2467600*. 2013.

Prabhu, R.K., and U.R. Rao. *The Mind of Mahatma Gandhi*. Ahmedabad, India: Navajivan Publishing House, 1998.

Puharich, Andrija. *The Sacred Mushroom: Key to the Door of Eternity*. New York: Doubleday, 1974.

"RAAF Captures Flying Saucer On Ranch in Roswell Region." *Roswell Daily Record*, July 8, 1947.

Randle, Kevin D., and Donald R. Schmitt. *The Truth About the UFO Crash at Roswell*. New York: M. Evans, 1994.

———. *UFO Crash at Roswell*. New York: Avon, 1991.

Randle, Kevin D. *Crash: When UFOs Fall From the Sky*. Pompton Plains, N.J.: New Page Books, 2010.

———. *Project Moon Dust: Beyond Roswell—Exposing the Government's Covert Investigations and Cover-ups*. New York: Harper, 1998.

———. "Roswell and Chase Brandon." *http://kevinrandle.blogspot.com/2012/07/roswell-and-chase-brandon.html*. July 10, 2012.

Randles, Jenny. *From out of the Blue*. New Brunswick, N.J.: Inner Light-Global Communications, 1991.

———. *UFO Crash Landing?* London, U.K.: Blandford, 1998.

Ravin, Carol. "Sybil Leek 1922-1982." *www.solsticepoint.com/astrologersmemorial/leek.html*. 2000.

Redfern, Nick. *A Covert Agenda*. London, U.K.: Simon & Schuster, 1997.

———. Interview with Freddie Wimbledon. July 14, 1994.

———. Interview with Matthew Bevan. April 12, 1998.

———. Interview with Nick Pope. March 27, 1998.

———. Interview with Nick Pope. March 29, 1994.

———. Interview with Robin Cole. September 29, 1997.

———. "Rendlesham: About Those Missing Files." *http://mysteriousuniverse.org/2011/03/rendlesham-about-those-missing-files/*. March 16, 2011.

———. "The Riddle of Hangar 18," *Planet on Sunday*, December 4, 1999.

Reich, Wilhelm. *Contact with Space*. Rangeley, Me.: CORE Pilot Press, 1957.

Reid, Tim. "Mystery of Watergate tape's missing 18 minutes may finally be solved," *Times*, July 30, 2009.

Report of the President's Commission on the Assassination of President Kennedy. Washington, D.C.: United States Government Printing Office, 1964.

Report of the Select Committee on Assassinations of the U.S. House of Representatives. Washington, D.C.: United States Government Printing Office, 1979.

Ronson, Jon. "Gary McKinnon: Pentagon hacker's worst nightmare comes true." *www.guardian.co.uk/world/2009/aug/01/gary-mckinnon-extradition-nightmare*. August 1, 2009.

———. "Jon Ronson Meets Hacker Gary McKinnon," *Guardian*, July 9, 2005.

Rose, Bill. "America's Secret Space Program...and the Super Valkyrie." *www.biblioteca pleyades.net/ciencia/ciencia_flyingobjects53.htm*. June 21, 2004.

"Rose Mary Woods." *www.nixonlibrary.gov/forresearchers/find/textual/central/smof/woods.php*.2013.

Ryan, Rosalind. "Bodyguard blames spies for Diana recordings." *www.guardian.co.uk/uk/2008/jan/09/monarchy*. January, 2008.

"S.L. MacGregor Mathers 1854-1918." *www.golden-dawn.org/biomathers.html*. 2013.

Schiff, Steven. Letter to Secretary of Defense, Les Aspin. March 11, 1993.

———. Letter to Secretary of Defense, Les Aspin. May 10, 1993.

"Searchers Fail to Find Object," *Tribune-Review*, December 10, 1965.

Sears, Neil. "Law chief to probe KGB agent's claim that David Kelly was 'exterminated.'" *www.dailymail.co.uk/news/article-1297444/KGB-agent-Boris-Karpichkovs-claim-David-Kelly-exterminated-faces-probe.html*. July 26, 2010.

"Self-Made Myth." *www.pbs.org/empires/napoleon/n_myth/self/page_1.html*. 2013.

Senate Select Committee on Intelligence. *Project MKUltra, the CIA's Program of Research in Behavioral Modification*. Washington, D.C.: August 3, 1977.

"Senators Condemn Mystery Spy Project." *www.msnbc.msn.com/id/6682352/ns/us_news-security/*. December 8, 2004.

"September 2008 Update from the Wilhelm Reich Infant Trust & the Wilhelm Reich Museum." *www.wilhelmreichtrust.org/update_08_09.html*. 2013.

"Sergeant Karl Wolf: 'I've Seen Classified Photos of ET Moon Structures." *http://newcrystalmind.com/2010/sergeant-karl-wolf-ive-seen-photos-of-et-moon-structures*. April 27, 2010.

"'Shaylergate' Explained." *http://news.bbc.co.uk/2/hi/uk_news/885588.stm*. August 20, 2000.

Simkin, John. "Maxwell Knight." *www.spartacus.schoolnet.co.uk/SSknightM.htm*. 2013.

———. "Sidney Gottlieb." *www.spartacus.schoolnet.co.uk/JFKgottlieb.htm*. March 2013.

Smith, Jerry E. *Haarp: The Ultimate Weapon of the Conspiracy*. Kempton, Ill.: Adventures Unlimited Press, 1998.

Spence, Richard B. *Secret Agent 666: Aleister Crowley, British Intelligence and the Occult*. Port Townsend, Wash.: Feral House, 2008.

Speriglio, Milo, and Steven Chain. *The Marilyn Conspiracy*. London, United Kingdom: Corgi, 1986.

Srinivasan, Kalpana. "J. Edgar Hoover death records getting another look," Associated Press, January 18, 1998.

Stern, Gary M. Letter to Jim Lesar, President, Assassination Archives and Research Center, *www.aarclibrary.org/notices/AARC_-_NARA_Leter_2012-06-12.pdf*. June 12, 2012.

Strieber, Whitley. "'Lost' UFO Files Tell a Chilling Truth." *www.unknowncountry.com/journal/lost-ufo-files-tell-chilling-truth*. June 16, 2011.

"Sukarno." *www.britannica.com/EBchecked/topic/572207/Sukarno*. 2013.

Summers, Anthony. *Goddess: The Secret Lives of Marilyn Monroe*. New York: Macmillan Publishing Company, 1985.

———. *Official and Confidential: The Secret Life of J. Edgar Hoover*. New York: Putnam, 1993.

Sutin, Lawrence. *Do What Thou Wilt: A Life of Aleister Crowley*. London, U.K.: Pindar Press, 2000.

Swann, Ingo. *Penetration*. Rapid City, S.D.: Ingo Swann Books, 1998.

"Sybil Leek—The South's White Witch." *www.bbc.co.uk/insideout/south/series1/sybil-leek.shtml*. October 28, 2002.

Symonds, John. *The Beast 666: The Life of Aleister Crowley*. New York: St. Martin's Press, 1997.

Symons, Baroness of Vernham. Memorandum. January 12, 2001.

Taylor, Rob. "Australia's military loses its UFO X-Files?" *www.reuters.com/arti cle/2011/06/07/us-australia-ufo-idUSTRE7560X420110607.* June 7, 2011.

Taylor, Matthew. "David Kelly postmortem reveals injuries were self-inflicted." *www.guardian.co.uk/politics/2010/oct/22/david-kelly-postmortem-self-inflicted.* October 22, 2010.

Telegraph reporters. "Doctors call for Dr David Kelly inquest to resume." *www.tele graph.co.uk/news/9861704/Doctors-call-for-Dr-David-Kelly-inquest-to-resume. html.* February 10, 2013.

"The Thirty Year Rule (but subject to exemptions…)." *http://politicalreform. ie/2011/12/31/the-thirty-year-rule-but-subject-to-exemptions/.* December 31, 2011.

Thomas, Gordon. *Journey into Madness.* London, U.K.: Corgi, 1988.

Thomas, Kenn. "Earth Vs. Flying Saucers With Cloudbusters." *http://silverscreensau cers.blogspot.com/2011_10_01_archive.html.* October 29, 2011.

"The Top Secret U.S. Military Space Program. Is the Future Already Here?" *www.abovetopsecret.com/forum/thread329997/pg1.* January 28, 2008.

Townsend, Mark. "The truth is out: X-Files go public." *www.guardian.co.uk/uk/2008/ jan/06/spaceexploration.military.* January 5, 2008.

Trudeau, Lieutenant General Arthur G. "Project Horizon Report: Volume I, Summary and Supporting Considerations." *www.history.army.mil/faq/horizon/Horizon_ V1.pdf.* June 9, 1959.

———. "Project Horizon Report: Volume I, Summary and Supporting Considerations." *www.history.army.mil/faq/horizon/Horizon_V2.pdf.* June 9, 1959.

"Truth about the Diana phone spies, by her guard." *www.dailymail.co.uk/news/arti cle-135106/Truth-Diana-phone-spies-guard.html.* 2013

Tuttle, Rich. "Senators Comments Suggest Evidence of Secret Space Program." *www. aviationweek.com/aw/generic/story_generic.jsp?channel=aerospacedaily&id=n ews/SECRET12134.xml.* December 13, 2004.

"U.S. Congress passes Espionage Act." *www.history.com/this-day-in-history/us-congress-passes-espionage-act.* 2013.

"UFO." *http://vault.fbi.gov/UFO.* 2013.

"UFOs and Marilyn Monroe." *UFO,* Vol. 10, No.2, 1995.

"Vladimir Pasechnik." *www.telegraph.co.uk/news/obituaries/1363752/Vladimir Pasechnik.html.* November 29, 2001.

Wagner, Stephen. "What's on the Far Side of the Moon?" *http://paranormal.about.com/ od/lunaranomalies/a/aa011507_2.htm.* January 15, 2007.

Ward, Mark. "History Repeats for Former Hacker." *http://news.bbc.co.uk/2/hi/technol ogy/4761985.stm.* May 11, 2006.

Warren, Larry, and Peter Robbins. *Left at East Gate.* New York: Cosimo, 2005.

Weaver, Colonel Richard L. *The Roswell Report: Fact vs. Fiction in the New Mexico Desert.* Headquarters, United States Air Force, 1995.

"Wilhelm Reich Infant Trust." *www.wilhelmreichtrust.org/.* 2013.

Williams, Lord of Mostyn. Memorandum. October 23, 1997.

Wilson, Jim. "The Dummies of Roswell." *www.popularmechanics.com/science/space/1997/9/roswell_dummies/index.phtml*. September 1997.

Wimbledon, Freddie. Letter to Nick Redfern. July 5, 1994.

Wolfe, Donald H. *The Assassination of Marilyn Monroe*. Soundings Ltd: Oxford, U.K., 1999.

Woodward, Bob. *The Secret Man*. New York: Simon & Schuster, 2006.

"Woomera Prohibited Area." *www.defence.gov.au/woomera/about.htm*. 2013.

"Yamasaki, Minoru (1912–1986), Seattle-born architect of New York's World Trade Center." *www.historylink.org/index.cfm?DisplayPage=output.cfm&File_Id=5352*. 2013.

INDEX

ABOUT THE AUTHOR

Nick Redfern works full-time as an author, lecturer, and journalist. He writes about a wide range of unsolved mysteries, including Bigfoot, UFOs, the Loch Ness Monster, alien encounters, and government conspiracies. His previous books include *The World's Weirdest Places*, *The Pyramids and the Pentagon*, *Keep Out!*, *The Real Men in Black*, *The NASA Conspiracies*, *Contactees*, and *Memoirs of a Monster Hunter*. He writes for many publications, including *UFO Magazine*, *Fate*, and *Fortean Times*. Nick has appeared on numerous television shows, including Fox News; The History Channel's *Ancient Aliens*, *Monster Quest*, and *UFO Hunters*; VH1's *Legend Hunters*; National Geographic Channel's *The Truth about UFOs* and *Paranatural*; BBC's *Out of this World*; MSNBC's *Countdown*; and SyFy Channel's *Proof Positive*. He can be contacted at *nickredfernfortean .blogspot.com*.